Lagom

*What You Need to Know About the Swedish
Art of Living a Balanced Life*

Contents

Introduction

The following chapters will discuss the Swedish secret to happy and fulfilling lives. It may go against a lot of what we value and are used to in our American culture, but with so many people searching for something more, something that will help to bring about more happiness, it could be just what you are looking for.

In this guidebook, we are going to spend some time looking at the Swedish lifestyle of lagom (pronounced "lah-gome"). This is a word that means "just enough". You do not want to have too much of something, but you do not want to go so much to the extreme that you will not be able to enjoy life either. With lagom, there are no extremes, we get just enough of everything that we want or need, and this leads to a happier and healthier life than ever before.

We are going to start out this guidebook by looking at what lagom is all about, and how it is meant to work. We will look at how you can add in "just enough" to your day and your life, and still gain so much more happiness than you would have ever imagined in the past. We will also spend some time looking at the benefits that come with lagom and why so many people are deciding to adopt the Swedish way of life into their own lives as well.

Once we have a better understanding of how lagom works and why it is so beneficial, it is time to dive further in and look at some of the different ways that you can add this into your own life. Lagom can be added into every part of your life, though this can seem a bit overwhelming to some people (just jumping right in), especially when they are used to the American consumerist lifestyle.

Therefore, it is perfectly fine to start out with lagom slowly. You can add it into one or two aspects of your life and notice a big improvement. When you are ready, and you see all the great benefits, you can easily add it into other aspects of your life, as you are ready. Along the way, this guidebook will provide you with the information that you need to really add Lagom to areas like your home, your work, your relationships, your food, your clothing, and even your style of parenting.

When you are ready to learn more about the Swedish philosophy of lagom, and you are ready to simplify your life to add in more happiness, make sure to continue reading this guidebook and learn more about how to get started.

Chapter 1: What is Lagom?

There are many different types of lifestyles that are encouraged throughout the world. And people, in different countries and with different backgrounds, may take life at a different pace than the rest of us. While Americans may seem to be moving faster and faster every day while feeling drained and like they have missed out on friendships and other things that are important, you will find that many countries, and even many people within this country, have decided to make a switch as well.

To start, we need to explore the ideas behind minimalism. Minimalism - which is basically the art of having less - is a big trend that has made its way into many different aspects of our lives including our home, our work, food, apparel, and so much more. We find that we may meal prep with fewer and more basic ingredients because it saves time and money. We learn how to cut down what is in our wardrobes to help make decisions easier and to reduce the footprint we are leaving on the planet. We stop buying as much stuff that we do not need so that our homes will not feel as cluttered in the long run.

While most of us understand what minimalism is all about and how it is meant to work. While consuming less is going to make us feel less debt to an item, we also need to explore more about this topic. Especially, we need to look at what minimalism means to other people, or what lagom means to other countries.

This brings us to our discussion of lagom. Lagom is going to be the Swedish art of balanced living. We can translate this word to being "not too little, not too much, just right." This may sound confusing, but it is a good way to help us stay busy and not become lazy, without having to take on too much in our work life, our home lives, and in all of the other aspects that seem to surround us on a daily basis.

As someone who is already a minimalist (or is at least thinking about becoming a minimalist), it is important to always do an evaluation of what is around you to see how much you can live without and still be comfortable, and even see what you are able to live without or how to live with less. The question here is: what if the issue we are facing is not continuing to eliminate or hoard? What it is more about finding the equilibrium that is perfect for our lifestyles without having to cause a lack or an excess in the process?

The idea behind lagom is not that you want to try to reach perfection. Instead, it is all about finding a simple and attainable kind of solution to the daily worries that you go through. This could include things like making sure you have enough downtime, eating better, reducing the amount of stress that you have, and even achieving more happiness. It is going to help us to learn how to balance work and life so that we can sustain it all and have them all exist harmoniously with one another.

This seems like a pretty practical and worthwhile kind of solution to our busy world, right? There are a lot of different things that you are able to do with this lifestyle choice, and we are going to explore a few of them throughout this guidebook. You will be learning more about what lagom is all about and why it is such a good option. The suggestions made in this book change be adapted in various manners to ensure that it works for your own lifestyle.

According to Linnea Dunne, the author of *Lagom: The Swedish Art of Balanced Living,* some of the different things that you can do in order to make sure that you are living this kind of lifestyle include working with ethical clothing, eating locally, trying to grow some of your own food, taking more breaks through the day to feel rested, and so on.

The thing to remember when you are working with lagom is that there are going to shift in our days and sometimes, no matter how hard we try, we are not going to be able to fit it in everywhere. This is part of the beauty of living lagom: if you cannot check everything off the list each day, that is not a big deal. Just keep the fuss out of the whole situation and make your day as fulfilling and relaxing as you can.

With lagom, you need to make sure that your aim is to have a fuss-free lifestyle. This means that we need to learn how to find contentment and pleasure in the things that we already have, even if what we have is not picture-perfect. Also, make your goal to understand how all the things that we do play an important part in how we are going to live a life that is less destructive, and more sustainable, on this earth.

Not everyone who decides to embrace the idea of lagom wants to be able to adopt it on a daily basis, doing it all of the time. It is easy to admit that going with a lifestyle that is free of all the stress and fuss probably sounds pretty ideal. In a culture where over-indulgence is going to be the norm and you are looked down on if you are not able to keep up with what the neighbors have, it is nice to think that there are many other methods that you can rely on. Lagom shows you how to sit back and relax, live with less stuff, and actually enjoy the life that you are living now.

When you first hear about this term, you may assume that it is the same as the popular "hygge" that was available a few years ago. It was almost impossible to head out anywhere or even enter a bookstore without seeing a lot of information on the Norwegian and

Danish word that meant coziness. There will be some similarities occurring between two ideas; hopefully you will be able to see through this guidebook that the lagom ideology is going to be a bit different.

While this term is going to seem similar, there are going to be some key differences. First off, hygge is going to be about coziness and being comfortable, and lagom is more about "just the right amount." The basic idea that comes with this lifestyle philosophy is that we need to find a good harmonious balance and the right amount of happiness. The goal is not having too much, but also not having too little in your life.

On its surface, hygge is more about taking time out and making sure that you always feel safe and cozy. Of course, while these two ideas are going to be a bit different, we can see how both of them are going to be able to complement each other nicely, and if you have already implemented the ideas of hygge into your life, or you are looking to get happiness, comfort, and less stress in all aspects of your life, then combining the two together can be the right answer for you.

We will also spend some time looking at the history that comes with lagom. The Swedes believe that the best way for anyone to live a happy life, they must follow the precepts of lagom. You deprive yourself of nothing, but you also make sure that you are not overdoing things. Moderation is the key here, and it is the best way for you to create a life that is balanced and fulfilling.

In fact, this idea is so indoctrinated into the culture of Sweden that it is visible in all of the different aspects of their life, from their work-life to their homes, and you can even find this idea in their political system. Everyone in this culture should have enough, but not too much – that is the essential principle that the people of Sweden stick with, and it ends up working great for them and their happiness levels.

Lagom is unique in that it strikes a nice balance between hygge and minimalism. You do not need to be heated up by piles of cozy blankets or burn the house down with all your scented candles! Likewise, you do not need to feel like you can only own one spoon, throwing out all the other things that you own. This is where lagom is going to be the best option because it allows you to meet in the middle between these two lifestyle ideas.

This is a kind of lifestyle that works so well because it is going to help leak over into all of the areas of your life, and not just one or two. Having a good work and life balance, having just the right number of possessions, being able to reduce the amount of stress that you have, and keeping a healthy amount of frugality are all essential. It can even go all the way down to eating the right amount of food at mealtimes and choosing the right clothes.

With some of these ideas in mind, it is now time for us to learn a few of the simple methods that you are able to use in order to help improve your life and ensure that you are going to use the ideas of lagom a bit better. Some of the ways that you can work on adding some more lagom in your life will include the following:

Adopt What is Known as "Morgondopp"

The first thing that we need to explore doing when you would like to add more of lagom into your lifestyle is to adopt the "morgondopp". Think about the landscape that comes with Sweden. It has been blessed with more than 7000 miles of coastline and at least 100,000 lakes. Because of all this water and the coastline that is near it, it is no wonder that the Swedes love to bathe! One of these bathing types is going to stand out from the rest, and that is the morgondopp, or the morning dip.

This process is something that the Swedes are often going to enjoy this between May and September when it is warmer, but there are some who are going to do this all throughout the year. This kind of bath is enjoyed first thing in the morning before they even have their first cup of coffee. The bather dons a dressing gown, then wanders down to the local bathing deck.

The length of time that you decide to stay in the water is going to depend on the temperature. Many people will start when the water reaches 50 degrees. Then they will jump right in and let the water wake them up and make them more ready for the day. It can be a humbling experience, and it is going to be relaxing to feel the cool breeze and the warm sun on your body when you are all done with that morning bath!

So, what are you supposed to do if you do not live anywhere near a lake, stream, river, or sea? A good place to start here is to end the daily shower that you take with a cold-water blast. It may not give you quite the same feeling as a saltwater swim, but you will still get many of the physiological benefits as well. If nothing else, it is going to help wake you up with a nice jolt!

Dare to Go Alone

Sometimes when you are practicing lagom, it is fine to do some things on your own. This sounds strange to many cultures that are outside of Sweden. We feel like we always need to be surrounded by other people and that if we are doing something alone, then no one likes us, or perhaps there is something else wrong. With lagom, sometimes it is just fine to go out and explore the world and do things on your own, without having a ton of other people around.

Consider trying something small to help you get started. You do not have to go crazy here and assume that the only way you can succeed here is to go out for weeks on end camping and exploring the wilderness. If this is something that is appealing to you, go ahead and do it. But for the most part, you do not have to take things to this kind of extreme. For those used to being around others all the time, maybe going out on a short walk in nature by your home - on your own - can be a good place to start.

Work on Your own Capsule Wardrobe

Another idea that we are going to talk about in a little more detail as this guidebook goes on - and in another chapter - is the idea of the capsule wardrobe. Loosely speaking, the wardrobe that you will find of the average Swedish person is going to be likened to what would be a capsule wardrobe. This is going to be a minimalist, highly practical closet that was created by clearing out any of the unused and unwanted clothes and replacing them with a limited number of loved and highly versatile garments that you could mix, match, and wear together if you like.

There are several benefits to this. It saves money on buying clothes all the time. Moreover, it makes it easier to pick out an outfit in the morning, or any other time, taking some of the stress out of your morning. In addition, it helps you to spend less time and energy on things like shopping and laundry. It is more economical, and those who decide to go with it are often going to feel so much happier in the long run.

Take Enough Breaks in Your Day

The Swedish time of fika-paus is a break with some coffee and sometimes a little treat. It could be an informal kind of catch-up with a colleague that was prompted by something like "Shall we meet up at 10 a.m. and have coffee?" Alternatively, it could be something that is a bit more formal, an event that you scheduled out on the calendar a long time in advance for everyone to get together. Whether it is more of a formal or an informal thing, it is going to include taking some time to "turn off" and have a breather, even if it is just for a few minutes.

In our modern culture, it is easy to feel guilty when we are going to take a break, and when we try to relax from all of the hard work that we do. But it is actually something that is good for you and can make you more productive. A study that was done at Baylor University's Hankamer School of Business found that those who took more breaks when they were at work reported that they had more energy, that they were able to concentrate more, have more motivation, and they were less likely to report some of the negative side- effects such as lower back pain and headaches.

What is interesting here is that the positive effects that come with these breaks are going to decrease the more time that you work between the breaks. This is why taking some short and regular breaks is the key to seeing success. In fact, if you want to practice some lagom, you should follow something like the 52 – 17-minute rule.

A recent study supported this idea, finding that those who were the most productive would work for 52 minutes, and then they would get a 17-minute break. While this is not something that many jobs are going to allow, it is still worth it for us to think about the frequency of our breaks and try to take some as often as we can in between our work.

This does not mean that you must go and talk to someone each time and have a long conversation. If you are more introverted and the idea of going out to find someone to talk to ten times a day seems daunting, then do not fret. Even having some time alone and indulging in a break on your own, can work just as well and will provide you with the same kinds of benefits.

Learn How to Listen More

If you ever converse with someone from Sweden, and you will notice that they are not going to waste any time interrupting or talking over another person. They keep their voices at an even tone, and it is acceptable to have some pauses in the conversation if needed. To those in American and other cultures, this can seem awkward. Culturally, we are so concerned about a gap in the conversation that we are going to jump in too soon, often trying to speak talk before the other person complete their sentence.

But in lagom, the idea is to stop and actually listen to another person. This helps to slow down the discourse and allows both parties to really feel like they are being listened to. It is hard to follow through will allowing the conversation with pauses; it can make us feel uncomfortable, and sometimes makes the conversation seem unnatural. We have been told that this is the way that we are supposed to behave and that the conversation has to keep going.

It is acceptable if the conversation flows back and forth with no stopping; trying to force this without really listening to what your other person is saying can be so bad for the encounter! Allowing for some pauses, enabling both parties to hear and process what the other one is saying, is so important. After all, the point is for both parties to actually understand what the conversation is about.

Perform Acts of Kindness

As with all the other topics that we have discussed with lagom, spreading happiness is something that you can easily do, without having to involve a ton of grand gesture. Sometimes a small and ordinary act will be enough and will mean the most when it inspires someone to smile in their day.

Even though you may think that you are a very caring person already, sometimes a gentle reminder to think of others and to remember to do something kind for them can go a long way. In addition, catching another person off guard with a bit of kindness that they were not expecting can be one of the most touching gestures of all. Some of the different ideas that you might think about using in order to get the most out of these random acts of kindness can include:

1. Leave a small note in one of the books that you are reading at the library to brighten someone's day.
2. Decide to give out ten compliments to various people throughout the day, ones that are heartfelt and genuine.
3. Write a thank-you note to the public service industry, such as a nurse, firemen, or the police.

4. Write a letter to a relative or a friend you have not been in touch with for a long time.

5. Carry around an extra umbrella or something similar, providing it to a friend in when they need it.

Living a life that is full of lagom is going to help you to improve your daily existence and your happiness. As you can see in this guidebook, it is a lot easier to accomplish than you may have originally thought. Taking breaks, thinking about others, stopping to listen rather than just react, and enjoying life rather than buying things and having to work to pay them off, can be so freeing to your overall life.

Chapter 2: The Benefits of lagom and Why You Should Pursue It NOW!

There are going to be many great benefits that you can receive when you decide to implement some of the ideas of the lagom system into your own life. This is why so many people have chosen to add in this kind of ideology to their own lives, ensuring that they reach happiness and then continue having a good life. It is in stark contrast to what we usually see when we look at our modern world, where we are encouraged to run around at a breakneck speed and just keep purchasing things left and right. With lagom, we learn what is just enough, but not too much, and it can lead to so much more happiness than ever before. With this in mind, let's look at some of the benefits that you'll reap when you decide to implement some lagom - even if it is not full time - into your life:

You Can Take Yourself Away from the Extremes

In our modern culture, we seem to go back and forth between the extremes. We go with either diet or bingeing. We spend time doing daily hard workouts or watching marathons on Netflix. These extremes are going to make us feel really unhappy and exhausted, and it is hard to know which way to turn. But the goal with lagom is to find a good medium, the medium of *just enough*. Just enough for play and work. A healthy diet with a nice dessert to enjoy when supper is done. Watching a bit of TV and then a good exercise during the day.

The balance, rather than taking it all away and depriving ourselves, is the essential ingredient that we should strive to remember daily with lagom. If we spend our whole lives trying to deprive ourselves of the things we should and need to do, or the things that we enjoy, we are going to end up on burn-out. After burn-out, it's easy to head the other direction, swinging to the other side of the pendulum; this is not good for us either.

The best way for us to really describe what lagom is all about, in just a few words, is it is the happiest grey area ever! This is a nice grey area where you are going to feel fulfilled by working out just enough, eating just enough, sleeping enough, and getting out there and adventuring enough. Gluttony is not the best for us at all, but this does not mean that we need to starve ourselves either. Working out all of the time is hard on the mind and the body but sitting around and never moving at all is not good for our bodies either. The grey area allows us to have just enough of both to be happy.

You Are Going to be Happier

Happiness can only begin when you have had a chance to get those basic needs taken care of, and it is going to end with the love and the gratitude of what your life is and is becoming. When you begin adding some of the principles of lagom into your life, you will see the importance of making sure that the excess is gone, leaving room for more of the things that are wanted and needed. When things are just right, which is encouraged with the fundamentals and process of lagom, you are going to feel good.

Our goal here is to not aim for giddy or over-the-top joy that starts by burning bright and then ends up fizzling out quickly like a fire that is started by gasoline with nothing to sustain it. We are, instead, shooting to reach a deep amount of contentedness and the joy that can last your whole life. Lagom is going to help you to reach this long-lasting happiness, rather than the quick joy that is going to be gone in no time. Lagom is meant to help you learn how to build a good life, rather than a life that seems empty and that has you searching for the next high.

How many times have you gone through life and found that you thought one thing, or another, would make you happier, but after the initial happiness, you found that it was not enough for you? The disappointment cycles, hitting you again and again. However, when you work with lagom, you are going to focus more on a type of contentment, and this is going to ensure that you can increase your levels of happiness. Moreover, who wouldn't want to increase the amount of happiness in their own lives?

You Will Become Healthier

Living in excess or in deprivation is never considered to be a healthy way to go about your life. Your mind and your body are not going to do that well when it comes to either extreme in the long term. By practicing lagom, you are going to help in maintaining some of your internal stability and will ensure that the mind and the body will be kept in homeostasis.

With lagom, you are going to learn how to do more of the healthy things that you need with balance. You will learn how to reach the right amount of working out, rather than doing too much and wearing yourself out - or too little, skipping out entirely on the health benefits of exercise. It is possible to have too much of both, so learning how to balance these can be so important.

Another benefit to your health with lagom is the improvement in your mental health. When you apply this kind of moderation to your life, your emotions and your brain are not going to fight against each other, and they will not feel quite as in flux as they may have before. Anxiety is often going to be caused by the individual feeling too overwhelmed on a regular basis. Stress is easily taken away when you add in some more moderation to your life, and almost every part of your body and mind can improve when you reduce your levels of stress.

Truly being able to apply the principles of lagom to your life can be helpful because it is going to ease your life. It allows you to have the permission needed to rest when you need it and know when it is time to work and get things done, as well.

Lagom is a Part of Being Mindful

When we are able to learn how to become more mindful, we are learning how to become more aware of the things around us. It is really as simple as that. To have the kind of moderation that is necessary to work with lagom, we need to be mindful.

Think about some of these following questions. How often do you get up to get a snack and then go back to the couch to watch another episode of your favorite show, just to find out that you have eaten the whole bag? Well, while this is something that all of us have done at some point in our lives, and this is certainly not what we are talking about when it comes to moderation! When we behave this way – eating too much of something like chips or cookies or some other unhealthy sort of snack – it just upsets our stomach, disrupts our usual diet, and leaves us feeling ashamed and defeated.

When we are considering the principles of lagom, we are going to learn how to add in some more moderation to our lives. With moderation, you are going to be more mindful. This is a tricky cycle to learn how to get just right, but it can really help you to reduce the amount of stress in your life, improve your amount of happiness, and make you feel like you have been able to level out your life a little bit.

Of course, we are not just talking about moderation and mindfulness when it comes to food. We want this to expand out to all areas in our lives as well. You need to learn how to be more moderate about your social media intake, your work, your relationships, with the levels of activity that you do, and more. It takes some time to add this into all of the things that you want to improve in your life, but starting with just one area of your life at a time and trying to improve as much as you can one step at a time *can make a difference.*

There are many different ways that you can add more mindfulness in your life, and there is no shortage of various techniques that you are going to be able to reach this mindfulness. Of all the methods and ways to reach a state of lagom in your life, you will find that one of the best ways is to reach that state of moderation and happiness is in this guidebook: mindfulness.

Mindfulness not only reduces some of the bad stress going on in your life, it also helps you appreciate some more of the small things that you already get to enjoy on a regular basis. Too many times, we are overworked and too busy running from one place to another, without any break in between, getting upset that time is passing too quickly. With the lagom idea of life - learning how to slow it down a bit and enjoying our lives becoming more mindful - we can really see and appreciate some of the little things that are there as well.

There Can be A Lot of Fulfillment in "Just Enough"

We live in a culture that is all about getting more and having more. We think that we need to have this thing and that thing. We go into debt to keep up with the neighbors and to have the best and the most of everything. This never makes us feel good for long; we are going to feel overwhelmed and tired and have to work more to pay off the things that we no longer need or even find happiness with. This is the exact idea that lagom works towards fixing in our lives.

To look at this from another angle, we need to be able to look at what lagom really is about. Lagom is partially about fulfillment. Living a life that is fulfilled is not about having the most for everyone; nor is it about having the least. Fulfillment is really just about finding the things in life that are going to help spark a fire in your soul and living in a way that will continue to help feed that fire.

Moreover, we do not want that fire to be around for a short amount of time and then disappear. We want to make sure that we can take that fire and keep it healthy and strong. To do this, we need to be able to find a nice balance between what you are putting into that fire to keep it going. Lagom is the perfect solution to help you maintain your fire and will help you to get there with less time - and less difficulty - in the long run.

This can a challenging thing to do when we are working within the modern American lifestyle. Americans seem to be all about more consumption, having more, and always going for more. However, this "more" is not what is making us happy at all. In fact, it is making us miserable, making it very difficult to ever relax, have free time, or even finding time to hang out with our friends and other loved ones in our lives.

A nice thing to consider: lagom and the way that encompasses the Swedish lifestyle could be the one thing that has it all figured out. It can help strike that balance between what our energies are being used for, without hitting extremes on either side. Life in moderation is one of the best ways for anyone to live, regardless of where they live, what they do, or what their interests are. Between the benefits that come with your physical and mental health – plus the mindset shifts that are going to be created by living a simpler and more moderate existence, lagom is going to be just right for your life.

With the belief in Sweden that everyone should have enough, but not too much, this could be one of the biggest reasons why Sweden, rather than America, is consistently rated as one of the happiest and best places to live. And it is mostly from this principle that we have already been discussing in this guidebook. While it may be hard to get started with moderation in the beginning (especially in the consumerist society that is so popular right now), we will see that making these changes and switching our mindset can be the trick that we need to live a much better life, one that is happier, better, and so much more worth living.

Lagom may be a process that seems somewhat foreign and new to a lot of us who are not from the country of Sweden, but it might be exactly what a lot of us are going to look for in order to improve our lives and find more happiness overall. It may take some shifting of your mindset and your way of living, but it is not as drastic and life changing as some of the other types of options that you can go with. That is one of the best outcomes that results from implementing lagom in your life.

Chapter 3: Adding Lagom into Your Home Life

The first place we are going to ta look in order to help you to really make sure that lagom is added into your life is in your home. You spend a good deal of your time in your home. You sleep there, enjoy time with your family, eat and cook there, take in some peaceful time, entertain, and feel safe and comfortable while you are in that area. It makes sense that you will want to spend some time adding in some more lagom into your life and you will want to start with this process in your own home.

There are a few different steps that you can begin taking in order to add in some more of the lagom principles into your own home. Of course, we need to make sure that we are going with "just enough" as the idea, and this can fall over into your decorating, and even the style that is present in your home. Remember that everyone is different, and this lifestyle is not going to ask you to conform to something that makes you act just like everyone else. Each person who adopts lagom is going to find that it can provide them with some good balance than they may not have had before, but they can still add their own twists to the mix.

To start, we need to take a look at some of the different décor tips, as well as some other tips that work well with the lagom principles. Some of the things that you can do to add more lagom into your home include:

Declutter the Home

To start with, decluttering your home can help to add in more of the lagom as well. A simple and balanced home is one of the best ways for you to achieve a lifestyle that is considered lagom. Not only does a lot of excessive décor all over the place start to contribute to the amount of anxiety that you feel (which can be bad for all parts of the body and mind), it is also going to block out some of your creativity, and can make it almost impossible for you and others in the home to relax.

The good news is that it is easy to declutter the home, and it is possible to do this without having to pay someone or spend a lot of money getting started on this. Start out by practicing lagom with the advice of "one in, one out" rule. This means that for each time that you buy and bring into the home, one item needs to go out. By practicing some small tasks on a regular basis, you will find that decluttering your home is going to be more manageable than ever before.

Choose White or Gray

If you are looking to get started with a new painting project in your home, then changing the walls to gray or white is the best choice for you. Both shades are good for brightening up space and can allow for accent pieces and any other items that you choose for that room to start standing out. In addition, the color palette is muted can really turn the home into a haven that is more relaxing to escape to after you finish up at work – or after completing all of the other obligations that you have during the day.

Of course, this does not mean that you are going to be stuck with just white and gray all of the time and that lagom isn't going to allow for other colors throughout the décor that you have. Instead, you should make it your main focus to create a sense of calm by avoiding brash or loud colors and patterns whenever it is possible in your home.

Bring Some More Nature Into Your Home

It is possible - and often encouraged - to use nature as a kind of accessory in your home. You can use a wooden table or use plants to help work with your decorations as well. Those lagom principles are going to lend themselves closer to minimalism than anything else, being able to introduce some nature into your home can be one of the best ways to brighten up space without trying to add in some more clutter. You can just add in some texture as well with a stone table or going further in any manner that you want, or just go through the process of introducing plants into your home.

Just having one plant in your home is a great way to help reduce how stressed out you feel. Even if there are not a lot of sunny windows in your home to support a plant, some great plant options that you can use are not going to require the same kind of upkeep as others. Options that you can choose to add into your home to follow this principle of lagom and to make sure that you are using plants that thrive with even a a limited amount of sunlight includes Madagascar dragon trees, leaf fig trees, spider plants, and aloe vera plants.

Let in some of that natural light

Given the fact that Sweden has a lot of long winter nights, the décor that comes with lagom is definitely going to focus on getting in as much of that natural light in your home as possible to give you more daylight and to warm the space up. When it is coupled together with a wall that is gray or white and you will find that the natural light is basically going to bounce around your home and can increase your happiness.

To achieve this kind of lighting, you can go with sheer window curtains and windows that are unobscured. These are good ways to make sure that as much of that natural light is able to get into the home as possible. If you are worried about how much privacy that you will have, but you would still like to follow along with this part of lagom, you can look for light and thin drapes that are going to let in some of that natural light that you want. You can also invest in some rolling blackout blinds for the nighttime so you can let that light in during the day and get more sleep at night.

Make sure that the objects in the room are able to breathe

As much as possible, try to set single items so that they apart from one another to give them some breathing space, as well as the spotlight that they really deserve. When you are doing some décor in lagom, each object needs to either serve a purpose or to delight you in some manner. In setting them apart from one another, it allows the room to feel less cluttered and makes it easier for you to appreciate the beauty and the purpose of each piece along the way.

Use some candlelight with a nice warm glow

Candles are going to be something that those who practice lagom are going to use on a regular basis because it helps to add in some of the ambiance to the room that they want. But they take this further than just using the candles in the evening. These candles can be featured at the breakfast table and even around the living room to make that area feel more welcoming and cozier at the same time.

It is important to fill your home with candles in places where you would like to add in a touch of light, such as in the center of the table or a dark corner. Work to balance the space, and make sure that shelves or another location is not going to be cluttered with too many candles in one place. Strive for equilibrium in your use of candles; instead of using too many in one place – or all over the place – set aside your extra candles so you will always have some on hand.

Replacing the carpets with rugs

Rugs are something that will be pretty common when you work on the décor of your home, as carpet is often considered as unhygienic. Transmatta, which translates to the term for "rag rug" in Swedish, will be a typical style that is seen within many homes. These rugs are made from scraps of clothing or old fabrics and are woven together using a loom.

If you are not able to find one of the transmatta, there can be some other simple rug styles of your choosing. To help you to create your own kind of makeshift carpet without dealing with some of the upkeep, layer rugs are going to be on top of each other, and can cover up the floor much like a carpet, but it will help you to take the rugs up and clean them easily whenever it is needed.

Mix together some of the modern and the vintage

Décor that is done in lagom is going to emphasize many things. It is going to mix together the comfortable ergonomic pieces with some of the vintage and stylish ones. This means blending antique pieces with modern ones and slowing down and searching for the best item to suit each space. Vintage furniture and some of the other décor pieces are going to be inherently lagom and in many cases, one person's trash can easily become the treasure of another's.

When searching for some of the décor and vintage furniture that you want to work with, make sure to have some patience. Measure out the space that you would like to fill, and then make sure that you are flexible in the process. You could go into a store and be imagining that you want one piece in your head, and then find that you run across something that is much better instead.

There are a lot of things that you can do in your lagom home in order to make it more comfortable and to ensure that it is going to be "just enough" to make you happy. Follow some of these tips to help you clear up your home and get it all comfortable and ready to go, and you will be well on your way to implementing more of the lagom philosophy in your own life.

Chapter 4: Adding lagom into Your Work or Office

The next place where we can add in a bit of lagom to our lifestyle is in the office. The Swedes do not just implement the idea of lagom only at home, they try to implement it into many different parts of their lives, ensuring that they can have that happiness in many different places, not just one. A collaborate approach and a work-life balance that is healthy is part of the Swedish mindset with work can even help a business benefit if they are willing to use the ideas of lagom as well.

Any employer who would like to create a place of work that is innovative and collaborative amongst all of the employees could really take some tips from the Swedish idea of lagom. The idea of "just the right amount" means that we need to favor things like collectiveness, balance, and moderation over hierarchy, overwork, and individualism. It may be quite a bit different than what we are going to see in an American culture, but it is still an appealing proposition to work with.

Being able to achieve a sensible balance between work and life for all employees is going to be important for any business, whether they are in Sweden, in America, or in many of the other countries on this planet. In addition, the 80-hour workweek is going to be unheard of when it comes to lagom; this long workweek would be counterproductive when trying to assimilate the ideas and processes that are embraced by lagom in your life. Working 80 hours a week or more may make you a lot of money, but between that and sleep you are not going to have time for family, friends, or even relaxation - all important in lagom as well.

For example, one Swedish start-up taking place in California avoids any monthly key performance indicators in the workplace. According to Lars Nordwall, the COO for this business, that this kind of target is going to force people to work long hours. As a result, they may cancel some of their own planned time off in order to get those performance numbers higher or to make up for any of the poor planning that may have happened during that time. This may sound good on the outside, but it results in a culture inside the business of mistrust, stress, and a lot of lack of motivation.

Instead, they like to follow what is known as an "annual operations plan", and the staff members there are included in the formation of this plan. We assume that people will work 40 to 50 hours a week, and that is it. The managers are coached and expected to refrain from asking for more from their employees; this is so that the staff does not experience a burn-out. This is done by making sure the managers, as well as the staff, plan ahead on things to ensure that they prioritize their workdays in a better way. This company even encourages the employees to take time off and leave the workday early on occasion.

The idea here is that the employees need to feel trusted. They do not need to be micromanaged all of the time, having someone overhead, monitoring them all every moment of every day, making them work 60 hours a week, and never allowing them to have a home life at all. This may make sense to the business owner who gets to take home a lot of money in the process, but it discourages employees, making them feel overrun and tired in the process, and this is never good for any employee - or for the company either. When an employee feels like they can be trusted, it is more likely that they are going to go above and beyond at any of the times that the business is going to need it more.

Think about it this way: if you are already working 60 hours or more a week, do you really want to add on more hours and more stress to take care of a business that is only interested in dollar signs and working you even harder? Or, would you put in more work and effort if you knew the business is valued you, letting you work just the 40 hours without guilt, gave you time to leave early if you had an appointment or wanted to take care of the kids, and didn't try to overwork you all of the time?

Another example of this is from Lars Bjork, an owner of a software business in Pennsylvania. According to Bjork, the only way to strike the right balance between work and home is to test and see what works, "swinging the pendulum," as he likes to put it. In this business, the staff has the option to work from their own homes instead of coming into the office all the time, and then they are allowed to experiment with their choice. The employees need to come in on occasion for some client meetings, but otherwise, they are allowed to work at home to help make things easier and to maintain a better work to life balance.

Another part of the lagom process that is found in the office is teamwork. This is why many companies created on this important principle are going to make decisions in a more collaborative manner. Employees are able to use various processes or attend meetings so that they are informed and can speak up on the process of making decisions for the whole company.

When an employee is able to make some of the decisions that affect the company, it is going to be really great for everyone. They know why certain things are going to be put into place, they can talk about the problems they see and try to make it better, and they can really work to feel less stress. They will feel like their opinions matter, even if they did not vote for all of the decisions that were accepted. In addition, because of their involvement in decision-making, the employees will feel less stressed out. Instances of mistrust, misunderstandings, and disputes are going to become much rarer compared to many American companies.

The goal with this overall idea is to come up with a consensus. Not everyone is going to be happy with all of the decisions all of the time, but the point is to strive for a consensus and as soon as the leader of that company or the group makes a decision, it is important that everyone in the business respects the decision and sticks with it. While the employees are asked to speak up and let their thoughts and opinions be known, it is also made clear in these kinds of businesses that the leaders get to come in and make the final decisions.

Therefore, with these is in mind, there are going to be a few different things that need to show up in a company and in your work life to make sure that you are adding in some of the lagom processes into it will include:

• Keep the work weeks to a minimum. When it comes to lagom, the 60 hours or more a week idea needs to disappear. No one is benefiting from this. It is simply resulting in employees who are worn out and tired, and who aren't performing as well as they should. Limiting the hours to 40 hours will be plenty for most companies and can result in employees who are more willing to go above and beyond when the time calls for it with their employer later on.

• Allow for some time to work at home. Sometimes, life comes up, and employees are going to need to be at home with a child, with their spouse, or because their car broke down. Forcing them to take days off and miss out on paychecks because of these life events can add to a level of stress that is not going to be good for them, or for your business. They miss out on money they need for bills, and you miss out on some of the productivity that is needed.

• Some businesses have started becoming more open in terms of the amount of time they allow their employees to work at home. This isn't possible for every business all the time and, of course, you may have to outline times when the employee needs to make it into work. That said, allowing some flexibility can ease the stress that your employees have, and can help you to still get the work done that you need.

• Do not have metrics that add in too much stress. Too many American companies spend their time coming up with hard metrics that they expect everyone to meet all of the time. They assume that with these metrics, they are going to be more productive and get things done. However, these just add in a lot of stress to your employees as they try to keep up, working harder and harder to meet the metrics.

• Instead, allowing the employees to have some say in the planning and in the metrics that are used can make a big difference. This will ensure that they can bring up some of their own concerns with the metrics that are being used and can help to ensure that the things that are being done are actually going to improve your business. You may be surprised by how much work can be done when you are not stressing employees out as much in the process.

• Allow for a safe and open environment for everyone. Everyone in the company needs to feel like they are valuable. Making them feel like they are only there to make the company money, and making it a big deal when they have to take time off, when they ask a question, or when they make a valid opinion, can really be detrimental to the employee, and to your business. Your business cannot run without the employees, so why treat them as if they should be machines that have no opinions or private life outside of the workplace.

• Consider listening to all employees when making decisions. Instead of having just one person in the business in charge of all the decisions (stepping on the toes of everyone else), why not consider having everyone involved make some of the decisions as well? Sure, it is fine to have one leader who can work to make the final decision, especially if there is not a consensus all of the time. However, when the individual employees are allowed to speak up and feel as if they are heard, it is much easier to make them feel as if they are a valuable part of a team, rather than just a number.

• Realize that your employees have - and want to have - a life outside of work. Employees like to go home and not have to worry about work. They want to have more time to go out, see friends, visit family, and spend time with their spouse and their kids. They do not like to have their employer calling them all of the time about an "emergency" that takes up hours of their life. In addition, they do not want to spend 60 hours a week at work and then spend more time on the weekends and at night trying to get more work done. They want to have the freedom to go home, turn off from work, and do the things that they like.

If you are trying to add more lagom into your life, this is the kind of job that you need to look for. Even if it may not be the highest paying job, finding one that allows you to take a breather, and not have to think about and do work all of the time, rather than the things that you want to do, can really help to improve your life and make it so much better overall.

In the American culture, most people struggle with the many issues of balancing a good work life with the rest of life. Many companies think that the best way to be productive and to get things done is to overwork employees, trying to get the very most of from worker. In the process of caring only about productivity, they have a high turnover or employees who are not motivated to do the job; this is harmful to the overall business.

Adding in some of the ideas that come with lagom can be one of the best ways to fix this issue. Including more freedom, reducing (or ending) all stopping all of the micromanaging, and cutting down on the long work hours can be the best way to have employees who are happy. There will still be plenty of – and likely more - productivity with the employees as well. Following the tips in this chapter will ensure that you are going to be able to see the best results with your employees.

Chapter 5: Lagom and Your Clothes and Wardrobe

The next part of lagom that we need to consider is how to handle your wardrobe and the clothes that you wear when following the principles of a lagom lifestyle. This includes learning how to keep your clothing and your wardrobe to a minimum so that you do not feel overwhelmed. Trying to keep up with all the costs of buying new clothes, as well as the expense of washing them all of the time, can be stressful. Now, we are going to spend some time looking at how you can make your entire wardrobe conform to the ideas of the lagom lifestyle, saving you a lot of time and money in the process.

The basis of a lagom closet is keeping the number of items down to a minimum; you do not need many items in your lagom closet. If you can barely get the closet door to open at all, then this is a sign that you are not living lagom at all! You want to have clothes that can be reused and changed up easily, clothes that are going to last, and ones that may work for formal and informal occasions depending on your needs. It is not unusual for the people of Sweden to go with just a few items of clothing and then mix and match them to get the looks that they want.

This can sometimes sound boring. You may worry that people will start to notice that you are wearing the same things all the time.

However, in reality, no one is really going to notice at all, and it is going to save you a lot of time and money. When you do not have to spend hours looking for the right outfit or trying to find something, and when you do not have to spend all that time washing your clothes, you can have the freedom to do other things. In addition, when you only need to purchase a few items to start with, it can really save you a lot of money as well.

There are a few things that you can consider working with when it comes to adding some lagom into your lifestyle. First, see if you can give your wardrobe a kind of facelift. As the fashion scene starts to move on and some of your styles goes with it, the way that you look at your clothes is going to change. Make sure that you go through your wardrobe on a regular basis, without making the focus passing things on.

You may be surprised at what is in the wardrobe, and what you would be able to wear again in a different manner. Maybe you find that you have an old skirt and see that it can now work perfectly as a quirky petticoat for an old dress that needs a lift. Maybe you can find some pants that you can rework into shorts and make them last a little bit longer.

The next thing to consider is dusting off that sewing machine. This is a great skill to learn; sewing can help you to keep some of your clothes for a bit longer and save money in the process. Maybe you start out by learning how to sew a button back onto a shirt, then you learn how to work with zippers, and possibly even learn how to adapt one of your own garments into something that is brand new. Consider watching some YouTube videos, and look into other similar learning options that can help make this a reality.

You also need to take some time to evaluate the capsule wardrobe that you have. Having a base of clothes that are useful (and that you enjoy wearing) can be great, but we need to consider this idea carefully; you may have a different idea of a capsule wardrobe than someone else. Maybe you have a base that has 11 floral-based dresses, while someone else wants to have a reliable range of trainers and waxed coats.

The next thing to work on is bravery: try out some of the matches which might seem ugly to you at first. It is something that may be hard to get started with, but it is really liberating to someone when you try something new out, get it wrong, and then just learn how to live with it. It is only by doing experiments that you are able to learn more about your own personal expressions, and you can become better at trusting your instincts when it comes to your style. Who knows, you may find that you fall in love with something that doesn't exactly fit the current trends? It's a learning experience.

There are also a few things that you can do to make your wardrobe more functional. Wardrobe changes will ensure that you have the outfits that you need, without all of the extras or unneeded pieces still hanging in your closet, taking up room. Some suggestions include:

1. Take good care of your clothes. Buying good quality helps your wardrobe to survive the rain and the cold, and even some of the hotter temperatures. Think about the long term with your clothes and get stuff that is higher in quality and will last longer – then take care of them! Yes, it may be more expensive, but if you can pick out a coat or a pair of pants that lasts for five or more years, rather than just one season, it is going to be much more advantageous for your wallet.

2. Forget what is going on with trends. When you follow lagom, and you go for the long term, you have to forget about the fads because these are short term and are going to change all of the time. Pick the style that you like, and then stick with this.

3. Put some of your comforts first. Nothing is going to ruin your day than going with shoes that barely fit or are not comfortable. You want to make sure that all of the items that you wear and put on your body are not just functional, but also comfortable so that you can make sure you are enjoying life more.

Changing up your wardrobe a bit when you are trying to follow lagom is sometimes hard. It is difficult to think about the long term when picking out the clothes that we want to wear, and sometimes it is easier to follow the trends knowing that we can change out of this all the time. However, with lagom, we think about comfort, we think about the long term, and we find items that are going to last us and will stick around and last us.

This is hard to manage sometimes, but it is going to be necessary to ensure that we are going to save money and have just enough. You may have to limit yourself on going out and purchasing something new all the time. Moreover, you may have to say no to things more than you would like. Nevertheless, the reward that comes with this is going to be so worth it in the long term and can bring you more happiness than ever before.

Chapter 6: Lagom and Your Food and Eating Choices

Lagom is something that you are able to work with when it comes to your eating choices. The American way of eating is not something that the rest of the world is going to share. Most countries are going to practice some more moderation when it comes to the amounts and types of foods that they eat. It seems in America that there is a lot of extreme; either people eat excessively and bring ruin to their health, or they eat so little that it can cause physical issues as well. However, with the idea of "just enough" that comes with lagom, we would be able to fix this kind of problem and learn to enjoy our food while maintaining our own health in the process.

When it comes to how you should eat, and eating well, lagom means that you should find balance; this means having an awareness of what your body actually needs, learning how to find your cues of satisfaction, and gauging how you feel as you are eating. This keeps things healthier and moving along better than eating until you are stuffed or only eating because it is time to eat, rather than what we think we should eat or whatever is on the plate.

The Swedes are often all about everything being in the right amount, but this does not mean that they are going to be afraid to treat themselves at times either. One only needs to take a look at all of the candy bins that are on the walls of all the stores in Sweden to see this. However, those who live in this country have a system for the treats, and they know when to treat themselves, and when to eat in a healthier manner.

For example, "lordagsgodis", which means "Saturday candy", is a tradition that has been around Sweden since the 1950's. The Swedish government (worried about the problem of dental caries in the country) recommended to parents that they give candy to their children only on Saturdays. To this day, if you are out shopping on a Saturday, you are going to see children out filling paper bags with gummy candies and licorice, even the kind that is saltier.

This can be a nice way to include a treat in your life. You do not have to completely give it up, but you learn how to limit it as much as possible along the way. You get avoid sweets and candies most of the time in order to keep your body healthier overall. Still, you'll have something to look forward to at the end of the week, and you can enjoy it in moderation, without giving it up all of the time.

Another option that you can work with is learning how to plate your foods. The Swedes like to take a more social kind of mealtime than what we are going to see with many American families. When it is time to eat (even at lunchtime in the workplace), they are going to place their food on real plates, and then sit down at a real communal table so that everyone will each lunch together. Sometimes there will be candles that are lit, and the conversation is going to include everyone rather than just one or two people talking to each other.

Unlike what many Americans are going to do during lunch, hardly anyone is going to eat out of a Tupperware container! You will not eat alone at your office; you will not go out to eat for lunch. You will not eat with just one other person and feel alone the whole time. In addition, you will not have to work during your mealtime either. This is all about working with others and having a break when it is time. Eating a meal that is plated makes it more formal and more of an event, and when you can actually leave your work behind to sit and talk with others at the table, it makes the experience so much better.

This is not just in the workplace, though. Those at home make sure that their meals are done on a plate as well. And even those at school or at a daycare are going to have their lunch plated and they will be seated at a table with a hot lunch, the right kind of cutlery, and a chance during the whole time in order to learn how to behave and use the right kinds of manners at the table as well.

This is something that takes a bit of time to grow accustomed to. Most Americans are used to rushing their lunch, trying to get it done as quickly as possible and not focusing too much on what they are eating (or how much they are eating!) They often eat alone and do not really enjoy their lunch because they know they are not really getting a break, often having to work at the same time, and missing out on the social experience that can come with it.

Once you make some of the changes, you will find that it really can be pleasant. Not only does this kind of eating more social, it is going to add some element of respect to the whole idea of eating - and eating well. Taking the time to plate your lunch on an actual plate and then sitting at a table with others (not at your desk) can turn the process of eating lunch into a more mindful act, allowing you to really enjoy the meal more than eating alone, eating at your desk, or while you are doing some work.

Another thing to learn when it comes to eating with the idea of lagom is that you do not have to fear fat. Letting go of a lot of the myths that are popular in America and eating things that have healthy fats in them can be a hard thing for many Americans who are worried about their diets and how healthy they can be. Still, this is something that you need to move past when it comes to eating in a balanced way on this kind of diet plan.

For example, those in the Swedish country are going to favor dairy that is full of fat, and once you get over the idea that all fats are bad, you will start to see why and enjoy this version over some of the others. But it is not going to end just with the dairy products that you consume though. Swedes enjoy having butter to be full in fat, cream sauces, and they will add in a lot of cheese to their meals – a lot more than you may be used to. This may be a lot different than what we think of as healthy, but it can be good for you if you do this consumption in moderation.

Even with this higher level of fat intake, it does not seem like the Swedes are overeating or gaining a lot of weight. This is because the right kinds of high-fat foods tend to be more satisfying, and good at helping you to not overeat, compared to some of the lower-fat options. If you learn how to listen to some of your own satisfied cues and do not take this too far, you would be able to lose weight and stay healthy the whole time, even when are eating foods that are higher in fat.

In addition to eating foods that are higher in healthy fats, you also need to make sure that there are a variety of grains present in your diet. Of course, there is going to be the regular kinds like rice and wheat, but when it comes to the type that most Swedes like to consume, rye is king in that country.

In Sweden, oats are going to be consumed in savory form, as an alternative to rice that is both more sustainable and more nutritious. Food oats, or Mathaver, are going to be chewier and thicker than some of the flaked or rolled oats that most Americans are used to working with, and it helps to make a better meal. Spelt is another common grain, as well, and can be eaten in many different forms and even baked into bread if you like.

Eating lots of healthy fruits and vegetables can make a lot of difference in the kinds of health that you are going to have as well. Try to add in some variety along with the other two food types that we have discussed. These are going to provide your body with a ton of great antioxidants and nutrients that the body needs and can be a great way for you to really get something sweet without having too much through the week and ruining the kind of moderation that you need.

Lagom is going to help us to slow down and listen to our bodies about how much to eat. If you are eating too quickly, it is hard to know when you are done with eating, and when you have had too much. Remember that lagom is all about *just enough*, so you should eat just enough to make the stomach happy and provide your body with the nutrients that it needs, and nothing more. But how are you supposed to know when you reach that point in eating if you have not slowed down enough to feel it?

Lagom is going to help us to actually enjoy our meals. Instead of going through and just scarfing down the food that you have all the time, without really tasting it or even remembering what you ate from one meal to the next, lagom asks you to slow down and actually get a chance to eat your meal and really enjoy it. This is so important for anyone who is trying to be healthier overall, and it can really make the whole idea of eating more enjoyable.

Slowing down, tasting the food that you eat on a daily basis, and being more mindful will make a big difference. You will enjoy the food that you are eating. You will slow down quite a bit and enjoy the mealtime as well. In addition, you will find that when you are able to slow down a bit, you can actually tell when you are satisfied, rather than overeating and then feeling – when it is too late - that it is time to stop.

Lagom is going to ensure that we eat more healthy foods that are better for us. Lagom is definitely not against the occasional treat. However, this does not mean that you should have so many treats that you are not being able to really watch the foods that you are eating along the way. Your diet should consist mostly of healthy foods, with lots of good protein, good whole grains and options, healthy fats, and good fruits and vegetables along the way. If you are able to eat these on a regular basis, you can then have treats on occasion – without the guilt!

Lagom allows us to turn our meals into a more social event, rather than hurrying through them. If you are used to eating alone all of the time, or you are used to eating at a desk while doing work, you probably already know that this is bad for a lot of different reasons. You are alone, which can be a bit depressing and does not allow you to get any socialization in. In addition, since eating at your desk often means that you are going to be working at the same time; this means you are not really getting a break in the process.

No matter what meal you are eating, lagom encourages it to be a social event. Sit down as a family and enjoy the breakfast together before you head off to school and work. Take some time during the workday to sit down with others in the office and talk, without excluding anyone, and be sociable. At night, either eat with your family or invite a friend over to enjoy a meal with you. These meals are not just about feeding the body and getting some nutrition in; they are also about taking a break from your day and improving your mental and emotional health AND becoming more social, all rolled up into one.

Lagom allows our meals to be more mindful. When we learn to focus on what we are eating in our meals we become more mindful of the food we are taking in. Take time to plate some of your meals rather than eating out of Tupperware or out of a bag. This helps the food (think fresh) as well as helping us to stop and enjoy the meals that we eat. Changing this one habit makes it easier to slow down and know when we are full, or when we are eating simply because food is in front of us.

It is important through this process that we learn how to actually listen to our bodies. In America, we see what the time is on the clock, and then assume that it is time for us to eat, whether or not we are actually feeling hungry at the time. When we fill up our plate, the plate is usually very large, and we feel like we need to eat every last bit, and sometimes go back for seconds.

While these things are going to help us to stay on a schedule, they are not going to be very conducive to helping us learn the signs and signals that our bodies are sending out, and it often causes us to eat excessively much. It's easy to see the truth in this concept; look at the rise of obesity and the epidemic that it is causing in America, and we see that this is definitely true.

With lagom though, it is important to learn how to cut out some of these habits, stopping them in their tracks. Eating too much food and filling ourselves past satiety is not a good way to maintain our health, and it is going to throw us off that balance that we are really trying to find in lagom. It may be the way that Americans eat, but most of us can agree that it is not the best way to do things and rushing through mealtime causing more harm than good.

The good news is that there are a few ways that you can change up your eating habits to make them fit in more with the ideas of lagom instead of sticking with the bad eating habits that you already have. To start, go with a smaller plate at mealtimes and do not fill the plate to the rim; this alone can cut hundreds of calories and will make you feel full when you are done.

While you are eating, take small bites and actually savor the food. This is where the idea of mindfulness is going to come into the picture and make things easier. After every two or three bites, take a drink of water as well. This helps to slow down your eating and keeps you hydrated so that you will not speed through the eating so fast. Often, we miss out on our cues of being satisfied because we are eating so fast, the stomach gets filled up before we can even realize what is going on. When we slow down, we can tell when we feel satisfied, and this is often going to be earlier than we even realize.

After you are done eating, do not go back for seconds. Your first plate is often going to be enough, and unless your stomach is still growling and begging for food, which is most likely isn't (so don't use this as an excuse,) you do not need to head back to get more food. Stick with the one plate and you are going to feel so much better.

When it comes to your mealtimes, mix things up as well. Just because you have gotten out of bed, or because it is noon does not mean that you have to eat at this time. This is what many Americans are conditioned for, but it is an unhealthy way to eat. It makes us feel like we need to eat at that time, even if we are not really feeling hungry. Learn how to read the hunger cues of your body and listen to those cues to tell you when it is time to eat, rather than the time on the clock. Depending on your own body, you may find that you do not need to eat as often as you thought in the past.

The idea of lagom is going to come into play many different ways when it comes to the way that you eat. It asks us to slow down a bit more so that we have a chance to really eat what we need, and nothing more. It asks us to have a chance to enjoy a meal with someone else, rather than always eating too much on our own. In addition, it asks us to enjoy some of the treats and the snacks that we want, as long as it is done in moderation.

This can be in stark contrast to what we are usually see with many of the eating habits in America. Nevertheless, when it is implemented in the proper manner, and we learn how to listen to our own bodies, rather than just eating because we think we need to, then we can see why lagom is such a good process for our whole health.

Chapter 7: How Your Holidays and Celebrations Can Be Improved with Lagom

No matter how much you like Christmas and all of the holiday spirit that comes with it, it is easy to admit that it has been taken over by commercialism – in other words: buying lots of stuff! Millions of Americans go into so much debt in order to really celebrate Christmas and all that comes with it, and this leads to many problems down the line.

The first issue is how much is spent on presents. There is a whole weekend, Black Friday and the days after it, that is devoted to big deals on Christmas presents, and trees are often filled to the brim with lots of different items for everyone in the family. Presents need to be bought for every person in the family, and even for some friends and coworkers and teachers and everyone else. It can cost a small fortune buying all of these presents, and many times even with all of the money spent, these presents will be forgotten about, broken, or in the way in just a few weeks.

The presents are not the only thing to be concerned about when it comes to the hassle with Christmas though. How much is spent on the lights around the house? How much is spent on a tree or on decorating the house, on all those Christmas parties, and all of the other festivities that come around this time? And how much time and money are spent to get all that food cooked and prepared to go see family and friends?

It is not that we do not enjoy these kinds of things, but it all sounds pretty exhausting, too. By the time the holiday is over, we all need a vacation from it, and our bank accounts are so drained that it takes most of the year in order to fix it and try to get things back in line. There has to be a better way to enjoy the good stuff of the holiday, without having such a mess to deal with along the way.

The good news is here that there are some other things that you can do in order to add more lagom into your holidays as well. Adding this into your holidays may seem like you are a bit of a Grinch, but if it helps to maintain your sanity along the way, takes away some of the stress, and helps you to keep to some of your budgets from being busted, then it is definitely something that is worth your time.

So, with this in mind, and remembering that we want to spend more of our time enjoying what is allowed in this holiday, rather than having to stress out and worry the whole time, we need to take some time to look at the different ways that you are able to add in more lagom into your Christmas and the other holidays that are in your life as well.

Christmas cards

There are a few different steps that you can take to handle these Christmas cards. Some people decide that Christmas cards have to be sent out to everyone in their family, and their friends and coworkers and other people they have not seen or talked to in years. They will make or find the best cards, send out hundreds of cards, take family pictures, get stamps, and so much more.

This can be stressful, especially when you stop to consider that people are not going to do anything with them once the holiday is over. This could definitely be a part of the process that you would keep out of your holiday time. It may seem like a hard thing to let go of, but when you don't need to worry about the stress of not getting a card to everyone, or about the cost and time that goes with each one, think about how much it is going to free you up and give you some time to enjoy the holidays!

The Christmas Decorations

The next thing that you can focus on in order to help out with the holiday season is with the decorations that you use during this time. If you really want to go with lagom, you would choose to not really have many kinds of decorations up at all, or just the minimal, like a tree and a few lights. However, some people are really into this holiday and enjoy having some more decorations around to celebrate. This is fine, but we need to find some simple and practical methods of doing this to ensure that we can really see the results and not have to go into debt or struggle at the same time.

There are a number of ways that you can make even your Christmas decorations fall into the realm of lagom. One of the best ways to help you can recycle the decorations that you have for this time of year is to pick out a Christmas tree that you are able to replant in the garden when you are done, or one that you are able to reuse year after year. Just make sure that when they are watered and moist the whole time that you keep them inside so that they are going to live until the holiday is over.

However, for those who do not have enough space to deal with planting a tree when the holidays are over, you may need to go with another option. You can purchase a real tree if you would like, but many people who take the lagom path will purchase a fake tree so that they can just reuse the tree from one year to the next. If you do go with one of the real trees, there are many municipalities who will pick up and dispose of the tree in the most ecological manner possible, and that is something that you should consider.

Another thing to consider is that one of the most lagom ways of decorating your home is to get foliage, branches, and even flowers from your own garden to help decorate the home and make it look good for the holiday. You can use any of the extra branches that you don't need from your real tree, or from the trees that you have outside: ivy, holly, and some of the other seasonal plants from outdoors in order to help decorate up the home, make the hearth and the mantle look better and to make the centerpieces that you need for your table.

You can add in other types of decorations if you would like but consider how much it is going to cost and whether you would be able to reuse it as much as possible. If you go with lights, get a high-quality kind that you will be able to use for a few years in a row. Pick out decorations either that can last through the whole winter, or that you can reuse at other parts of the year without a lot of extra work. The more that you are able to reuse things and make them work for the other things that you will need in life, the easier this process will become.

The Wrapping Paper

We are even able to take some of the wrapping paper that we are using and make it work for lagom as well. You may not realize it ahead of time, but it is possible that a lot of the wrapping paper that you try to send to the green bin cannot be recycled, especially if you find that you go with some that have glitter finishes, is metallic, or has plastic on part of the surface.

An idea that is much better for you is using brown paper to make your own wrapping paper. You can recycle this later. Consider adding some tinsel or using some pretty string; use your imagination to help make your own wrapping paper unique and unusual. Doing this adds a personal touch, giving a unique look that you are not able to find with any of the commercial wrapping papers that are out there.

There are a few different ways that you can do this and even save money in the process. You can keep some of the old paper and bags that you get from the grocery stores and use this for your wrapping paper. If you save the old bags and keep them for a bit, then this is the perfect way to wrap presents without having to spend any money in the process.

Alternatively, you can choose to give up the wrapping paper altogether and go with something like a fabric bag to wrap up some of your presents. You can often find a lot of old pieces of fabric at your home or at a thrift shop and can make a bag that you are able to reuse repeatedly.

The Meal

If you are having a meal at your home for the holiday or throwing your own kind of holiday party, then it is likely that the sheer amount of work that you have to put into it is going to seem overwhelming. It can get expensive to spend your time getting plates, decorations, silverware, nice things for the whole process, and to make all of the meals, desserts, and sides that you would need in order to really have a nice party.

You do not have to go through all of this process and feel so stressed out in order to have a nice holiday with some of your friends and family. You just need to know where to cut back and where to work hard to make it nice. First, if you insist on cooking the meal, there are a few options to have. You can cut down on the number of sides and desserts that you are going to cook. Choose just one meat that you are going to cook, instead of three options. Alternatively, even ask others to bring along a side, a condiment, or a drink to help. The more hands who are able to help, the easier it is going to be.

Another option here: if you do not feel comfortable with asking your guests to bring in their own foods and parts of the meal, try having your meal catered. There are a lot of affordable options out there with some unique offerings as well, and this can help to cut out some of the stress, allowing you to enjoy your holidays, while still providing your guests with a good meal.

Many times, those who are throwing these kinds of parties are going to worry about every little detail and hope that it is all perfect. However, in reality, your friends and family are there to have a good time and to see you; they are not going to worry so much about all of the little details. Who really cares if you are using paper plates or real China? Who cares if the plates and the cups and everything else actually matches? Having things a little different and a little less formal can make the party that much more fun.

In addition, here, you need to consider how much you can actually take on when it comes to the holidays. Many people like to hit everything during this time, in the hopes that they will be able to squeeze out everything from the holiday, and that they will not make anyone mad. But before they know it, their holiday is stuffed full of parties, school events, work events, caroling, cooking, and so much that they can't sit back and relax and actually enjoy the holiday that they are in. This means that too much is going on, and it is definitely a sign that some lagom needs to be added in.

Before the holiday is even set to start, it is a good idea to take a step back and actually take a look at what is going to come up, and what is the most important to you. Stuffing one or more social events into each day is not a good idea, and definitely is more than enough for anyone to handle. Sure, you can still accept invitations to things, be social, and enjoy the season. However, your time should not be so packed full that you are stressed out.

During this time, before accepting an invitation, consider whether it is something that you would really like to do and really enjoy.

Consider who is throwing the party or get-together, how you would feel if you could miss it without making anyone mad and think about how stressful it might make that day for you. In addition, when all of these factors are considered, you can *then decide* if it is worth your time to go to that outing or not.

Christmas presents

The final thing that we need to take a look at when it comes to adding lagom into your holiday time is with the Christmas presents. When it comes to these, we need to take a step back and consider whether we really need to go all out and buy so much for the year? How many of those items do we actually need? In addition, are some gifts that are actually going to be used on a regular basis by your friends and family and your kids, or is it something that is going to be thrown out and never used again?

Yes, it is always a lovely idea to give and receive gifts, but maybe it is time to really consider the giving that we are doing, and not just give out presents for the sake of it. This ensures that the gifts that we do give are more meaningful, useful. Another advantage to thinking through the idea of present-giving: this helps us avoid just picking out the first item we see, spending too much money, in the process.

The best thing that you can do here is to set a budget with the idea of frugality as the main aim here. You may find that *giving memories rather than things* can be so useful to help you to have a better Christmas, without spending money on a gift that is going to be worthless to the other person in no time at all. You could give out a voucher to do something for the other person or to go somewhere with that other person. Always remember that giving your time is a much better present than any item that you are going to use. You can also consider making a present for the other person as well.

Yes, you will have children who will ask and beg for the latest and greatest thing all of the time. This is nothing new, but it is not something that you need to give into all of the time. You can limit some of the gifts that they get that are just going to be underfoot in no time and work with this instead, giving the experiences and time rather than giving them more things that are going to be in the way again.

Remember here that the idea of lagom is not to get rid of everything, but to make sure that you have just enough when it comes to the different parts of your life. This ensures that you can still enjoy the holiday that is coming your way, rather than stressing out and worrying about all of the different parts of the holiday that make you feel overwhelmed with too much responsibility. This can take some adjustment, especially in light of all of the commercialism that comes with being in America. Still it is one of the best ways to ensure that you are going to be able to really enjoy the holiday and spend it with the people you love, doing some of the things that you really love. And isn't that what we all really want during the holidays?

As you can see, it is possible for you to take the holidays, especially with Christmas, and add in some lagom to it. In fact, once you get over the idea that people are going to judge you or that you are going to miss out on something important during the holiday, this gets easier. You will find that adding in lagom - doing just enough rather than too much during this time of year is - going to make a world of difference in how much you will actually be able to do and enjoy when it comes to the holiday season.

Chapter 8: The Lagom Parenting Style

It is even possible that we are able to take some of the ideas that come with lagom and apply them to your experience and your work as a parent. Parenting is really hard; there are so many opinions and parenting styles that it is hard to know what is going to be the best one for your needs. In addition, it always seems like one person thinks that their style of parenting is going to be better than what someone else is going to have. How do we know when we are parenting in the proper manner, and how can we add the ideas of lagom into the parenting?

Although it is true that parenting is going to be a matter that is very personal, and it is going to vary based on the family dynamics and the children in the family. Many parents are going to decide that it is worth their time to incorporate the lagom beliefs and elements into some of what they are doing when they raise their own children.

Something that may not be that surprising here is that many of these ideas are going to come from the way that families in this country raise their children. Similarly, they may be based on concepts that are becoming really popularized throughout the rest of the world. If you would like to learn more about how lagom can be used in the realm of parenting, and you want to figure out how you can add this into your own home, and into some of the things that you are doing with parenting, there are a few suggestions that you can follow.

Let us start with something simple. You want to make sure that your child is getting enough natural light and natural air as well. This is important no matter what stage your child is in at the time - even as a baby. Whether this means getting them outside to play and enjoy what nature has to offer, or if it means opening up the windows and letting the air in while they play inside and take a nap, then this is what you need to do.

In Sweden, most of the doctors there are going to recommend all of this natural air and light in order to encourage the child to develop a healthy immune system and to feel happier. Of course, if your baby is dealing with some health risks that opening up the windows while napping could aggravate, then, of course, you can avoid this suggestion and go with something else in our list of parenting choices. This is also something that you can discuss with your doctor to figure out if it is right for you and your child.

The next thing that you can add into your parenting style when you are working with the lagom parenting style is that you should spend as much time as you can with your children while also maintaining some balance. Families who live in Sweden make a practice of spending time together often, and they will even be happy to take a long and extended vacation together without it seeming off or out of the ordinary. Parents in Sweden are going to spend a lot of time playing outside with their children and will have a good deal of interest in what is going on in the lives of their children.

This may be quite a bit different than what we are going to see when it comes to an American family. Most of these families are going to spend a lot of time apart because the parents are working. The parents will sometimes go out with the kids, but often the kids are going to be on their own and more independent. This is something that would not be seen when it comes to the lagom lifestyle and the lagom type of parenting.

On the other hand, it is also important for us to keep things as balanced and as in check as possible, and we have to remember that while spending time with our children is important, they are individuals. Children should have their own private time away from their parents and other family members on occasion too. It is important to spend time with them, but respect the boundaries that your children have, depending on their age.

Remember that, in lagom, it is acceptable to work with childcare if it is needed. In Sweden, it is common for the parents to send their children to a childcare facility from an early age, and it is not really something that is going to be frowned upon when you need to get back to work after having a baby. Daycares in Sweden exist in many variations, and there are going to be a lot of options out there for a family to choose from based on what seems to be the best for them.

One thing to remember, though, is that while the daycare is just fine if it is something that works the best for your child, you still need to set aside some time after work and after daycare in order to spend some one-on-one time as a family with your child each day. This helps to keep that bond strong and will make sure that all of the emotional needs of your child are being met, even when you spend the day at work.

For a true lifestyle that is considered lagom, children need to have some encouragement to play outside on a regular basis. Parents also need to make sure that they are getting as involved in this as possible and should either be active with their children when the child is outside, or the parent should remain close by while the children are outside playing.

There are a number of reasons for this suggestion. It can ensure that the child is going to be safe while they are playing and that if something goes wrong, there is going to be someone nearby who will be able to help them out and comfort them. If something goes awry, the parent can fix the issue. Plus, spending time together, especially in the outdoors as much as possible, is going to help the whole family on many levels, including on an emotional level.

When you play outside, get more active, and have a lot of access - or at least as much as possible - to play in the fresh air and in the sunshine, this is going to become a very important part of working with the lagom lifestyle. In Sweden, it is not uncommon for families and their children to play outside, no matter what the weather is doing; families make a point to play whether it is snowing, raining, cold, warm, and everything in between.

As you can see, working with the ideas of lagom parenting are going to be a bit different than what you may be used to when you work with other forms of parenting. It is not really helicopter parenting because it recognizes that the child needs to have some independence and has to be allowed to do things on their own, without a parent on top of them all the time. That being said, it also gives another opportunity for the parent and child to bond, helping to create a close family unit. It is important and it is only going to grow stronger when the family can spend some time together and work to reach a common goal.

This is something that is going to seem a bit strange and hard to comprehend for many American families. It seems like we go between the two extremes in many of the things that we do. A parent is often either on top of their child and being there all of the time, giving the child no time to be an individual. Conversely, American parents go to the other extreme, never being around the child, hardly ever spending time with the child. The idea of lagom parenting is going to help us to find a happy medium that occurs between ends of this spectrum - which can be beneficial to the parents and to the child.

No matter whether you spend time at work, or you get to stay home with your child, it is important that you spend some time as a family unit each day. Go to the park and spend some time playing. Do art projects or some other craft together for some time. Go on longer vacations together and really sit back and enjoy that time that you get to spend together.

By the same token, it is also acceptable – and encouraged – to let your child go free some of the time. If your child wants to set a boundary or is looking to do something that requires them to be alone on occasion, then this is fine. You do not have to be connected at the hip to your child all the time. You just need to let them know that you are always there to love and support them and that you are their biggest fan. Recognizing that they will and do have their own lives - and they want to enjoy this as well - can ensure that they know they have that support, while still being able to grow and develop on their own.

The lagom parenting style is a lot different from what many families in America may be used to at the time they read this. It asks for a good balance to happen between what the family does together, and what the child is able to do on their own. As we discussed earlier, most families in American seem to fall on one end of the spectrum or the other: they are either fine with giving the child all of the independence that they want with no family quality time together, or they will be helicopter parents who never let their children grow and explore and mature on their own.

Finding a happy medium between this can be hard. You want to be able to have that quality bonding time as a family, without a lot of distractions and other things going on, and you want to make sure that your child has a good base to come back to when they need love and support. But you have to also mix this in with your child wanting to be an individual and really get a chance to take off and do his or her own thing. There is no right or wrong answer with this one. But learning what the balance is for your family and for your child is going to make all of the difference.

Just remember, you do need to make sure that whether you are home all day with your child or you work outside of the home and need to send them somewhere else for the day, that it is *your job to actually spend some time with your child*. The amount of time that is necessary is going to vary based on the family, but do not believe that a quick "hi" at the end of the day is going to cut it. It needs to be some high-quality family time - whether that is a taking a walk together, making dinner together, talking, reading, or doing something else that no one else is going to be able to interrupt and get in the middle of.

During the rest of the day, it is fine if the child wants to be a bit independent and do some of the things that they want, on their own. They may want to spend time with their friends; they may want to get into a sport or another kind of activity. Alternatively, they may just want to have some time on their own at the end of the day to pursue their own hobbies and to have some alone time. Allowing for this individualism, along with some open arms for the child to feel loved and supported can be so important as well.

This balance is something that is hard to do and stick with all of the time. But you will find that over time, and with some patience along the way, that this is easier to handle. You and your family have to spend some time figuring out what works best for you. Maybe you and your family like to spend more time together, and only a little bit of time as individuals doing your own things. Alternatively, maybe you like to spend more time doing individualistic things and then coming together at night to share and be a family.

Always remember that the experience of lagom is not going to be the same for everyone who decides to use it. Some people will take a different path than what you may have considered for yourself. This does not mean that their method of using lagom is any better or worse than yours. Adding in some of the lagom parenting tricks and learning how you can really live a happy and fulfilled life with your children can change the way that you view raising your children.

Chapter 9: Lagom in Your Love Life

It is even possible to put some lagom in your love life! This is a place where a lot of people would like to see some improvement, but it is hard to find the right balance when starting a new relationship. You may be busy impressing the other person enough that they are willing to go out with you and start a new relationship; this does not leave you with a lot of time to manage all the other things going on in your life at the same time.

It is a big balancing act to make everything work out the way that you would like, and even when a new relationship is started, you do not want to be stuck in the trap of having one thing take over all of the other aspects. In addition, with the ideas that come with lagom, you will find that you are able to manage this a bit better, giving you a better chance at romance, and a better love relationship overall as well.

Keep the Dates Simple

There are too many people today - thanks to social media and the other aspects that are going on around us - who are trying to compete all of the time. They have to have the biggest dates, get the biggest rings, and do the most daring stunts, just to impress someone and even get started on the date, much less what they need to do for the rest of the relationship.

If all of this already exhausts you, and the thought of having to keep coming up with new and bigger ideas of how to impress others and keep the relationship going, then lagom may be the right thing for you. There is nothing wrong with a grand gesture on occasion, but often the best grand gestures are the small ones that mean the most to you as a couple. When you let go of the idea of all doing all these grand things you think you need to do for other person, just focusing on the two of you as a couple, you will find that it is much easier to have a deeper and a meaningful relationship.

This can go all the way to the kinds of dates that you have as well. While a fancy restaurant can be nice sometimes, having to do the greatest and the best each time is exhausting and expensive. Why not a walk and a picnic, or even just have a nice date night at home with homemade food and a nice movie? This helps to take some of the pressure off both of you and can be a great way to talk and get to know one another.

Remember with lagom that it is going to be all about the balance and how the two of you can create a possible new life together as a couple. In addition, if you start out being out of balance in the first place, it is going to become even harder to gain this balance back later on in the relationship.

Do Things that You Both Enjoy

As you are working on building up a new relationship, it is important that you learn how to do things that both of you enjoy. You do not want to be the only one having fun on all of the dates or the other things that you do! You also do not want to be the one who is bored along the way either. When the two of you do things that you both enjoy, it is much easier to have fun and create a lasting bond that is so good for the relationship.

This may include, at times, going out of your comfort zone and trying something new. Maybe you each take turns picking out the activity and getting the other person to go along with you. However, there still needs to be some balance present to ensure that everyone is getting the attention and getting a chance to do what they want as well. If one person in the relationship is taking over and controlling all of the dates and everything that happens in each one, then there is a big imbalance that is going to show up in that relationship, and a lot of the lagom that you are trying to create in your life, as well as in this relationship, is going to start failing.

Take time out for each other

The next tip concerns the fact that you should take a break from one another and do things on your own on occasion. This tip is going to reveal how it is so important to actually make sure that you are scheduling out time for one another. No relationship is going to grow or flourish if one or both of you are so busy with the other activities in your life that you can never spend time one on one with each other.

This is sometimes hard to do in our modern world, and often it may feel like we are balancing a million plates at once. However, if it is needed, bring out your schedule books and write down a time, just as if you would with any other important meeting. Whether you need to do this once a week or a few times scattered out when it works for you, setting aside some time on the calendar will ensure that you are going to actually see each other.

Your relationship has to fit into the balance with lagom on occasion as well. Even if we do not mean for it to happen, sometimes the other distractions of the world and the other things that we need to take care of on a regular basis are going to bring us down and can make it hard to do this. It is so important for a relationship to grow and flourish by spending time together, so start adding this as something important that needs to happen in your own relationship today to maintain that lagom balance.

Understand that "Alone Time" is Just Fine

When you get into a romantic relationship, it is sometimes easy to let yourself go a bit and want to spend all of your free time with the other person. You want to talk to them all day long, you want to call them, you think about them at work, and you cannot wait to get off and go spend more time with them. While this is something that commonly happens with new love, we have to realize that it is creating an imbalance that is not good for anyone.

Think of how much is being missed out on in the other parts of your life. Your work is likely suffering because all you can do is think about this other person. Your friends and family are getting pushed back and may feel a bit neglected and like they are not as important as this new person is, and they may feel a little left out and abandoned as well. While this is probably not what you had meant to do, it is something that can happen if you are not careful.

This does not mean that spending time with the new love interest in your life is a bad thing. In fact, it is necessary for the relationship to grow and flourish the way that you would like, and for both of you to learn a bit more about one another. However, when it becomes obsessive and includes the two of you only ever spending time with one another, then it is creating an imbalance that is definitely not a part of lagom.

It is perfectly fine to take a break from one another on occasion. Yes, you love each other and enjoy spending time with one another, but there are other things in your life that you need to balance out as well, even when you are married. You need to spend time with your parents and siblings, and maybe even other friends. You may need to go to a work function on your own on occasion. You may want to take some time to do a hobby or just do something on your own and think of how much anticipating you will have when it is finally time for you and your partner to get back together after the short break!

Go at a Speed that is Right for Both of You

Sometimes, we are so caught up in the romance of something that we want to just jump right in and take full advantage of it to move things too quickly. When both parties want to do this and have settled on it being the best course of action for both of them, then this is going to be just fine, and you can move ahead. Remember that the *just enough* can be different for each person, and for each couple as well. Maybe moving faster in the relationship is what works and is just enough for this couple. *Maybe not.*

However, you are bringing two people in the relationship, and while just enough may be fast (or even slow) for one person, it may not be enough (or too much) for the other person. In a relationship, the feelings of both parties must be taken into account. If you are pushing someone to move faster and they do not feel comfortable with it, then this is going to cause some stress and anxiety in the process. In addition, if you are holding someone back, despite their efforts to wait for you and consider you, this can cause some of the same issues in the process as well.

This is why both parties need to be in agreement, and lagom can help. It is very important to spend time talking honestly about what is valuable to you in the relationship and where you are feeling the relationship should go in different stages. In addition, being open-minded to what the other person is saying is going to be critical as well. It is not enough to just say your piece, and then expect the other person to agree. When both parties can be open-minded and pay attention to what the other is saying, they are going to find that it enhances their relationship and makes it stronger. They can work together to find the just enough that is good for both, leaving them able to put the stress behind them and grow and develop a strong and lasting relationship together.

Even the relationships that you have with other people, and in your romantic life, can use the ideas of lagom. You can have a nice time with one another and build up a good courtship with the help of the just enough philosophy, rather than going over the top and having to worry through how to impress them, how much it is costing and more. Moreover, in the long run, it is going to create happier and more lasting relationships overall.

Chapter 10: Can Lagom Save You Money?

It is possible for lagom - when it is used in a proper manner - to even help you to save some money. This may seem a bit strange and may sound like a wild claim. However, when you learn how to live with just enough, rather than with too much and lots of excesses, it is going to result in you being able to make do with less, and that alone will save you money.

The idea of lagom is not to go through your home and throw away everything until you have one pair of clothes and a few dishes to work with. The idea is to just learn how to have a nice balance with things. You can purchase things - but purchase them because they bring you happiness and contentment, rather than because you feel jealous that someone else has them or an advertisement convinced you.

There are a number of ways that the process of lagom is going to be able to help you actually save money, and they are pretty simple. In fact, just by following some of the other tips that we have already spent some time on in this guidebook, you will be able to work with lagom in a manner that helps you to save money. Some of the other methods that you are able to implement into your day-to-day life that will ensure that lagom is being used properly and can help you to save some money include:

Purchase Fewer Things

With lagom, you are going to learn how to purchase fewer things. You do not have to give up on everything that you want to purchase, and you do not have to live your life like a hermit in order to embrace the ideals of lagom. That said, it does require you to learn how to just live with what you need, rather than having a ton of stuff that does not even bring you happiness and ends up just cluttering up your home, making a mess.

It is hard to learn how to live with less in our society. More is seen as better and the more that you have, the more that you can impress others and get them to pay attention to you. This stuff just results in clutter all over the home, and that clutter has been proven to cause anxiety and depression. Just remember having all that stuff means you have to pay for it, maintain it, store it; if you paid with credit, you have big bills and lots of debt to pay off. It is no wonder that you have to work all the time!

That cycle needs to stop. This is in excess, causing us to get out of balance and away from the *just enough* mentality that we should have with lagom. This can be hard, and there are many people – including the marketing team for big companies - that work hard to tell us that we need more stuff. However, we can live with less, and probably be much happier in the process.

Eat Less

The next thing that lagom can help you out with when it comes to saving money is the idea that you are going to eat less. The American diet is full of lots of food, and portions that are not going to be to properly scaled to each consumer's size, or consist of healthy options as they need to be. We spend a large amount of money on the food that we eat; between the grocery store and eating out, the snacks and everything else, it just does not take long before we start to see a lot of our money go down the drain – just for food.

When you decide to live the lagom lifestyle, you learn to eat just enough, rather than too much. This alone is going to save you money because it helps you to learn how to cut out the excess of food that you consume and focus more on just eating what you want. Think of how small your grocery bill is going to go when you can implement this into your own life.

Plus, with lagom, you are less likely to eat out as often, though you can still do this on occasion. However, your goal is more being responsible with your money and doing things in *just enough* fashion. Therefore, the eating out on a regular basis, or all of the time like many Americans, would be out of balance; you need to stop doing this altogether. This could save you quite a bit of money all on its own, especially if you and your family spent a lot of time eating out during the week.

Learn to Spend only on What is Important

One of the best things that you are going to learn when you start implementing lagom into your life is to spend your time and money on ONLY the things that are important. Lagom is a bit different than minimalism, as lagom ideals are not about focusing on getting rid of everything; lagom's focus is living with less. You will certainly try to downsize when you are going through this kind of process, and you learn how to not purchase as much in the future, but the focus is not going down to the bare minimum. It is more about finding a balance between purchasing just to fill a void and purchasing things that will make you happy.

For example, say you are an avid reader. One of your hobbies is reading, and you love to pick out a new book, even if it is from an old bookstore. You enjoy flipping through the pages to see what is there. Perhaps you decide to cut out on some of the other stuff, like eating out, having the latest technology gadget or something else, and spend a little extra on some of the books that you want to read.

Alternatively, maybe you like to travel and make memories with your family. Therefore, you choose to cut out the eating out, and you keep everything to a minimum so that you can afford to travel as much as you want. The trick here is not to deprive yourself all of the time. Finding what is important to you, and what is going to make your life a bit happier, is going to be the key.

No one is going to go through this process in the same manner. You may like books, while someone else likes to travel, and another person likes to paint or listen to music or do something else. You have to do what is important to you. Maybe you want to get serious about your debt, cutting back as much as possible and working to get that debt paid off. *Just enough* is going to be different for everyone. Cutting back on some things, and just spending a little bit on the things that are the most important to you can really do some wonders for helping you to save money - especially on things that were not really that important to you in the first place.

Learn How to Pay Down Your Debts

While we are in this process of embracing the lagom way of life, it is often recommended that you learn how to cut down on some of the debts that you have. The American lifestyle and idea that we need to buy more in order to be happier has certainly put a big dent in our credit, causing us to take on thousands of dollars in debt. This is often seen as the way of life at this time; we are supposed to have debt. We feel that we cannot get a car, a home, a college education, or pay for Christmas without having a credit card and lots of debt to handle it.

The truth is, we can live without the debt and without the credit cards. We simply need to learn how to work with *just enough*, rather than living in excess. Do we need to go to a private four-year university and take four or five years to go to school, or could we go to a public in-state college - or even a technical college - and save money? Can we find ways to keep our car going for a bit longer and save up for a nice car, rather than having to buy the newest car model that just came on the market? Does Christmas need to cost thousands of dollars, or can we do it for a lot less, giving gifts that are more thoughtful and more meaningful?

When you work through lagom with your spending and your budget, you learn that you can easily be happy on less, and you will not have to spend as much money. Moreover, this can give you some extra money to throw at the debt on a regular basis. Before you know it, your *just enough* attitude and way of living has helped to pay off some of the debts you owe, making it easier for you to save up a nice nest egg, do more traveling, and enjoy the life you have even more.

Learn How to Ignore Commercialism

Ignoring the commercialism out there is going to be one of the most important - although one of the most difficult - things that you have to do when it comes to implementing lagom into your life and making sure that you can use this idea to help save some money. This commercialism is all around us. We see commercials and other advertisements saying that we need to get this product or another product in order to feel happy. We see our neighbors and family members purchasing something that may make us feel a bit jealous. We may even see things on social media, like people getting new homes, going on vacation, and more and we feel jealous – leading us to believe that we need to be doing some of the same things as well.

This is a dangerous mindset to get into. These things are not going to make us happy at all and are just going to make it feel like we are always behind. We may get a bit of happiness at the beginning from those items, but it will not take long before that happiness is gone, and we are looking for the next high. Before we know it, we are going to have a house full of stuff, a lot of clutter, and we have to work more and more in order to pay off the debts that we took on for those items.

This is not going to lead to the happiness that we want, and since it is adding in some more stress because of all the extra work that we need to do, we can tell that this idea of consumerism is not going to be the best for our needs. We have to learn how to cut out some of the things that are going to try to draw us back. Whether we learn how to cut down on the social media intake, we turn off the television and not watch all those commercials, put down the magazines, or learn how to fill out a contentment journal (designed to help us to feel happier with the things that we already have in life) we have to learn how to cut out some of that consumerism and live with *just enough.*

Learn Difference Between a "Want" and a "Need"

Another thing that you are able to learn more about when you decide to implement the lagom lifestyle is the idea of a want and a need. These are two different ideas; a need is something like the food you eat and the home you live in. A "want" is everything else, such as the special clothes you want to have, the books, the expensive car, and more.

Lagom is not asking you to get rid of everything that you own and never purchase a single thing. However, it can help you to save money because it allows you to learn what you really need, rather than having you just go out and purchase things because you see it in a commercial, or because a friend has that item, or for some other reason. This can help you so much!

First, it is going to save you money. The less that you go out and purchase the more money you are going to save. When you stop spending money on items that you don't even need, not only will it help you to save some money, but it will ensure that you will be able to decrease the amount of clutter in your home, giving you more peace and happiness in the process as well.

Our consumerist society is not always going to be the easiest to fight against. We are tricked into thinking that many of the purchases we make actually fill our *needs*, when actually they are only "wants." This can make it hard to keep up with all of the different products and purchases that we think we need to have, and this makes life difficult to work with sometimes. However, setting some goals, and remembering the idea of lagom and "just enough" can be a good way to help you be prepared along the way.

It is possible to use lagom to help you to save money, as long as you are willing to fight against some of the commercialism that surrounds us all. It is possible to live a very happy and productive life if we just learn how to live with just enough rather than thinking we need all of the latest and greatest things all of the time. This is hard to do sometimes, especially in a society where more is seen as best. When you are practicing lagom, you can let go of this trap, the trap of purchasing more items, then having to work hard to pay for those items that no longer bring you joy or happiness after a short amount of time, and then doing it all over again. When you use lagom to help you regulate yourself and take in just enough to help you feel happier and more complete, you can definitely save money while also improving your quality of life.

Chapter 11: What About Hobbies That are Considered Lagom?

The next topic that we need to take a look at when we talk about lagom to help improve your life is how it can pertain to your hobbies. While you are taking some time to relax and do the hobbies and other activities that make you happy, it is still important that you can add in some lagom so that you can achieve a good level of balance all in one. You may even decide that you want to take up a few new hobbies that are considered lagom, especially if you feel like something you spend your time with right now is not quite right or is not giving you the happiness that you crave.

We always have to remember as we go through this process that lagom is going to be all about finding a balance. Whether this balance is in our work life or with our family and friends - and even with our hobbies - it is so important to add this to our lives as much as possible. Finding the best kind of balance that we can between work, time with our friends and family, and time to spend doing something we love is so important. Our hobbies are going to be such an important part of all of this!

No matter what you like to do as a hobby, it is important for you to make sure you keep things in balance each time that you try to enjoy that hobby. It is tempting sometimes to spend all of your free time on the hobby, but this is not a good thing for you either. It is better to choose a variety of activities to help you create a true amount of balance in your life. You also do not want to take it so far that you focus on work and nothing else, neglecting to give yourself plenty of time to enjoy all of those hobbies that you love.

If you can, you should consider bringing others into the hobby that you love. You can encourage them to do the hobby with you, do some new hobbies with them to learn something you may not have considered before, or even just show them what you have been working on. When you can share in a hobby with another person, you are able to balance doing your hobby with spending time with those you appreciate and love. This is a fantastic way to add in some more lagom to your life.

Another thing to consider here is that your work should never get to the point of becoming your hobby. Many people, especially those who own their business or who work from home, have a hard time separating our work and the hobby, and sometimes these are going to turn into the same thing. This may be tempting and easy to do, but there need to draw some distinct lines when it comes to what your work is, and what your hobbies are.

A hobby is something that you actually enjoy doing, something that gives you a lot of joy and happiness, not something that is going to bring you a lot of stress. If you take the time to do your hobby and you feel stressed out by doing it - or while doing it - then maybe this is not the right hobby for you to do. It is time, when the stress hits you, to take a step back and look at another kind of hobby that you can do while you emotionally process the source of the issue.

You will find that this process of separating yourself from the stress and emotional issues that come with your hobbies, is actually showing you that your hobbies are inadvertently becoming your *job*. This is why is it is so important to separate these two from each other. You need to have a good amount of balance between the different parts of your life and focusing on having the hobby and your work as the same thing is not going to achieve this balance at all.

Of course, we need to always remember that when we are picking out the hobbies that we are going to insert into this part of our lives, we need to have some of the relaxation hobbies included into the mix. You may be interested in doing some options that are different from this, but if you work with one of the old familiar hobbies, you may find that this not only brings you enjoyment but also helps you to relax a bit in the process.

For example, if you enjoy building things, you can try some woodworking. You can take up drawing or painting if you feel like you want to be creative. Alternatively, you can opt for something like crochet, sewing, or knitting if you would like to have a hobby that is fun and easy to bring along with you anywhere. Sometimes these seem like the old-fashioned and boring choices to make, but when they come to the lagom lifestyle of balance and adding in some relaxation to your life, they are great choices to make.

The good news here is that you can to have complete control over what you add to your lifestyle and what kinds of hobbies you enjoy. If none of the above suggestions sound like they are going to work well for you (or you cannot get into them), then do not stress out. Pick out a hobby that works for you. The goal here is to do something that you love, something that brings you some enjoyment and does not stress you out in the process. If you are able to do this, then any hobby that you choose is going to be just fine.

As you are picking out the kind of hobby that you want to work with, remember that you need to remain frugal. It is so easy to overspend when starting out on a new hobby! The whole point of working on this hobby is to bring yourself some enjoyment and to maintain the *just enough* philosophy as well. You do not want to go into a lot of debt in order to get started with the new hobby or to restart one of the hobbies that you are already doing. If you are worried about balancing your budget and making a new hobby fit in because it costs thousands of dollars or more, then this is going to add stress into your life and will not be the best option for a lagom lifestyle.

It is fine to spend a little bit of money on the hobby to get started, but keep this to a minimum, and be thoughtful and careful about how much you are spending. You do not want any unwanted in your life, so it is going to be imperative that you carefully consider the expenditures involved with your hobby. This is part of the lagom way of life, and your hobbies have to be held to the same standard as the other parts of your life, as discussed in this guidebook.

Remember that lagom is all about balance and *just enough*. Your hobby needs to bring you happiness, peace, and relaxation as much as possible. Spending a lot of money on the hobby and stressing out about how much it is going to cost you will not help you to reach the amount of happiness and fulfillment that you are looking for. It is just as bad as picking out a hobby that is not enjoyable or right for your needs.

Yes, it is possible that you will enjoy and pick out a hobby that is more pricey, such as collecting classic cars, but you still need to take the time to find ways to limit the costs, and create a budget and stick with it when you make any purchase. This is part of your new lagom life. You do not want to go into a large amount of debt for your hobby and then have to go through and work more and throw all of the other aspects of your life out of balance just for this one part.

For example, maybe you set aside a little bit of your income each month in order to purchase the supplies that you want for this hobby. Alternatively, maybe you decide that you do not really need to have all of the hobby-related items that go with it. You can get along nicely with some of the most basic items and be good to go. If you feel that you need one of the items for the hobby, consider writing it down, and then waiting a week or two. Then come back to that list and see how you feel about buying the item or items. You may be able to cross a few items off the list, realizing that they are not that important, and you do not really need them in order to work on that hobby.

Don't stress too much about this part either: Remember that you do not want to have this hobby stress you out because of it not being fun or the costs taking too much of your income. Focusing on something that you enjoy, and something that can take you away from some of the worries and stress that come from work and other aspects of your life can be very important to add in the balance that lagom requires.

There are so many hobbies that you can choose to add to your lifestyle and enjoy, that it makes sense to add them into your life and actually take some time for yourself. This may seem strange or unusual in the American culture but taking time for yourself is not a selfish action. Doing this can actually help you to improve some of the other relationships that you may encounter. Take some time to discover what your hobbies are all about and see how great this can be for your own life and adding in lagom as well.

Lagom can reach into all of the different aspects that come with your life, and this is going to include the hobbies that you want to work with. Picking out hobbies that bring you lots of joy - and even ones that can be done with others you know and love - can be so important to helping you to fulfill your life, reduce the stress, and add in more happiness than you may be able to get from your work life or other areas. While taking some time for yourself can seem selfish and hard to handle in the American culture, it is actually really good for you. By following some of the tips and suggestions in this guidebook, you will be able to enjoy your hobbies in the lagom way.

Chapter 12: Can I Add Lagom Into My Life with Pets?

Having a pet in your family can be a great experience. Whether you have had this family addition for a long time, or this is an animal you have just introduced into the family, a pet can bring a lot of fun, a lot of love, a lot of happiness, and even a lot of peace. Moreover, having a pet can certainly be a part of the lagom lifestyle if you choose. When considering your pet, make smart decisions about how you are going to handle the pet, the stuff you get for the pet, how and what you will feed it, those costs, as well as other considerations. Whether your pet is a dog, a cat, a fish or some other family friend, the suggestions in this chapter will make sure that you get the full enjoyment that you can out of this family friend, while still living the lagom lifestyle on a daily basis.

Even when it comes to your furry (or scaly or feathery) member of your family, it is possible to add in some of the ideas that come with lagom. Pets tend to bring in a lot of joy rather than not, but they are also able to bring in some stress to your life on occasion as well. Keep this in mind while you check out some of the suggestions that we are going to discuss through this chapter so that you can learn the best methods of incorporating lagom into the way that you treat and keep your pets

Just like with some of the ideas that we talked about with parenting earlier on, you are able to create a nice balance in your life; consider this for your pets as well. The proper way that you should discipline and train a pet may be difficult for everyone to agree on, but for many cases, it is best to practice rewarding good behavior in your furry friends. Getting into this kind of habit right from the beginning, when you first bring the pet home, can help to balance out their behavior a lot, and can bring in some more calm to the whole household. In addition, when the other people in the home can be calm and collected around the pet, this can translate into the personality of your pet as well, making life so much easier.

With this in mind, it is time to look at a few of the other things that you are going to be able to do in order to handle your pet and actually enjoy them, rather than worrying about them being too active or adding more stress in your life. The first thing that you can do here is to get out and enjoy nature with your pet. This is especially important if you have to spend some time at work; your pet may feel a bit neglected during those long absences.

Spending a bit of time on a walk or outside with your pet helps you both to enjoy nature and allows you to get some fresh air at the same time. Walking your dog is a great activity for both of you because it helps you and the pet bond, gets you outside into the fresh air, and can encourage you to be more active. The dog or cat (or ferret, or whatever) is also going to enjoy this because they get to spend time with you, while also burning off some of that extra energy they have from being stuck inside all day.

Now, there are times when a dog or another pet you are dealing with is going to run into some behavioral problems; this is to be expected. If this is something that you have been dealing with in your pet - especially when it comes to destroying items and chewing on things they should not - most therapists that work with pet behavior will encourage you to start out by walking the dog on a daily basis, right when you get home if possible.

The reason that this is going to be so successful is that often the dog is acting out because either they want some more attention to you, or they want to be able to get out some of the excess energy that they have from being trapped inside all day long. The walk is going to help with both or either of these two problems, and you will be surprised at how much of a difference this is going to make in how well your pet behaves.

If you are working with a cat that stays indoors or another kind of pet that is not able to go outside, there are still steps that you are able to take to ensure that this pet gets a bit more nature in its life. For example, if you have a fish tank, or another container with a turtle, snake, or lizard living inside of it, you could do some research to find plants that are safe for your pet and can be put into the tank. This is a safe and effective manner to bring some of outside nature into your pet's surroundings.

Let us say that your pet is a rodent and they are not able to head outside or enjoy any soil or plants; try opening up a window that is near them for at least a bit each day so they can get some fresh air. Just make sure that you are not trying to do this when it is too cold outside, or when there might be a chance that the pet is able to escape out of the window and go exploring on their own outside without you.

Just like with the other parts that come with lagom, you have to remember to always practice balance, especially when it comes to the choice about whether or not you should bring home a new pet to your family. Some people find that this is *just enough* to complete their family and make things so much better and happier. On the other hand, some others find that it is just too much work and stress for them. If you want to bring home a pet because it seems like the right choice for you, then go ahead and do that. However, if you are bringing home a pet because you feel that you are obligated to, or because everyone else has one, then this is not lagom. In this case, it is best to leave well enough alone.

Also, if you are a big animal lover and feel a big tug on your heartstrings to take in every needy or stray animal that you see, be aware that this is not lagom. It may be a noble thing to do and shows your big heart, but it is going to be stressful and too much. Caring for all of those animals is not going to be the *just enough* that lagom is trying to promote! Also, consider that this is going to cause such an imbalance as your home gets taken over by clutter, destroyed by animals, and overrun in a manner that you cannot control. This does not sound relaxing at all!

While having a pet is a perfect way to add to your family and can certainly be the way that you add some more lagom into your life, it isn't necessarily something that you want to go overboard with. For some people, it is something that you don't want to do at all. Learning what is best for your family, and having just enough in terms of pets (whether this is none, one, or more) can make a difference; they must fit in with the lagom lifestyle that you are trying to build.

Chapter 13: Lagom While Traveling

Another topic that we are going to spend a little bit of time discussing when it comes to lagom is the idea of how lagom can work when it comes to traveling. Many people love to travel. Whether it is a quick visit to go and see a family member or a friend, or something that is meant to be a vacation with the kids, or on your own, to some place that is new and exciting, a vacation can be something that we can implement into the process of lagom.

Planning a vacation is sometimes going to be a mixed bag. We are excited about the journey and where we are going, but trying to plan all of the details, such as where you should stay, what to see, how to get there, what to eat, and more can be a big hassle sometimes. Planning all of this and coming up with a budget to cover it all - especially if you are taking yourself and the kids - can give you a headache and often makes you wonder if it is worth the trouble and the stress in the first place.

The good news is that you are able to do the traveling and create all of those great memories at the same time! Let's dive in and see some of the steps that you can take in order to make this happen while maintaining your lagom lifestyle.

Taking a vacation from work can be a good thing because it helps to create more of a healthy work-to-life balance, and for many people, it turns into an extremely relaxing experience. On the other hand, as we discussed a bit before, it can take a lot of planning and execution in order to make the vacation all work out, especially if it is to a location that you have not been to in the past. All of this comes together to be extremely stressful in the process.

Traveling, depending on the methods that you use to do so, can be a strenuous time for not only you, but for the whole family. Remember, the whole point of this is to have some time together, to take a break, and even to bond with one another along the way. This is what every family wants when they decide to travel together and have some fun, but sometimes, the plans aren't always going to work the way that we think they should, and this can create a lot of anxiety, discontent, and - of course - anger in the process. The idea of lagom, if it is used in the proper manner, can help to fix all of these problems and give you the family vacation that you are dreaming about.

Practicing lagom throughout your travels, as well as the whole time that you are actually traveling, can help you to stay more focused, help you to relax, and ensures that you are able to keep some of the mindfulness in your life as well. When you are able to bring all of these different parts together at the same time, they help you to form some stronger and longer-lasting memories of the experience and the vacation as well. Some of the tips that you can use to help make your travels more fun and relaxing while adding in some lagom to the experience are discussed below.

Make some plans to help you stay organized, but do not stress out if you are not able to stick to them exactly for one reason or another. Things are going to happen in life, and no matter how well you plan and try to keep on schedule things are not always going to turn out the way that you would like. If you do not add in some flexibility to the plans, then you are going to end up with grumpy kids, anxiety in you, lots of fighting, and so on, just because of a little shift in plans.

For example, be sure to plan ahead in terms of scheduling the transportation that you want to take to get to your destination, such as a train a bus or a plane. You should also take some time to plan ahead to figure out where you are going to stay the night, such as which hotel you are going to use when you do get to your destination.

However, even these things are going to change. The plane may take off late and you will not be able to get to your destination at the time you had planned. Alternatively, you may find that the hotel you wanted to be booked up too fast and you now need to make some changes to get to the right location and have a place to sleep. Stressing out about this because it goes against your plans is not going to be a good idea and can start to taint some of the good memories that you are trying to make. No matter how hard you try, things are not always going to work the way you want, and you will have a much more enjoyable time if you can take a step back and relax, rather than feeling dark and disappointed because things did not work out.

Outside of some of the necessities that we talked about above, try to keep most of the schedule loose and flexible. You can go and do some things as you would like to but realize that you don't need to be there at a certain time; leave things open in case someone is tired and needs a break. It is also a good idea to allow some downtime in the day, just hanging by the pool or at the hotel room, so that you are not rushing around the whole time.

Now, there may be times when you want to leave the country to do some of your own exploring and to have more of an adventure when you travel. Before you go, maybe consider bonding with your whole family as you try to learn a few keywords and phrases that will work in that country and in their language. You can also try out new foods in the area and visit some of the important landmarks while you are there

Always make sure that you are practicing the right kind of balance, and make sure that everyone in the party is respectful when it comes to visiting with cultures that are outside your own. You may not fully understand why a culture would want to take part in one practice, or why they like a certain food or holiday, but you can still learn how to be respectful and learn about their culture, rather than causing problems.

If you plan to head out to a destination that is going to be pretty hectic the whole time, such as a major theme park or a beach that is pretty busy, then you should also plan some time to take it easy and relax into your day. If you can, set aside time when everyone can get away from the hustle and bustle and take a nap as they wish, or even have them just sit down and read or listen to their favorite music rather than having all of that stimulation.

Yes, being at a theme park can be a lot of fun, and there are always a million things that you are going to be able to do while you are there. However, these experiences can have so much stimulation that i puts you out of balance, and your energy levels are going to deplete so quickly - much faster than they will do at home. Having this break to recharge is going to be a great way to balance yourself out again after all that noise, those sights, and everything else that is out in the amusement park. Taking small breaks can help you to feel better and ready to take on more during the day.

It is also possible to take a vacation that is meant to just be relaxing and nothing else. You may assume that to go on a vacation you need to be out there, planning a ton of activities and running around the whole time to get the good memories. However, this is just not the case. It is going to end up causing you a lot of stress and headaches, and while it is sometimes fun to have a good plan, other times it is nice to just take a vacation, sit back, and relax during it.

Never underestimate the idea that it can be vital and so important for you to just spend some time together om a new location, with some different scenery, rather than having to be home all the time. Even planning a big vacation can cause a lot of stress! Consider renting a big cabin in the woods together and hanging out with your extended family. Alternatively, maybe hit the beach and just have fun with the water and the sand and something good to eat and drink along the way.

These are just a few examples of what you can do when dealing with a true lagom experience when you go on a vacation. There are too many families who are trying to make things perfect and planning every part of the whole vacation. While this may be done with good intentions along the way, it is not going to encourage the fun and the bonding that these trips are supposed to have, simply because it causes too much stress and too much anxiety on the whole family. Let go a bit, just be flexible, and realize that the most important thing to do here is to just spend time with your family and have some fun. If you can do this, then you are well on your way to having a vacation that is balanced, fun, and going to help you to create some great memories.

Going on a vacation with your family does not have to be a lot of work or hard or anything like that. It is meant to help you to have fun and take a break from all of the work and other obligations that you meet on a regular basis. A vacation helps you to create the bonds and the memories that you want with your children as they grow up. With the help of lagom and some of the different options that we have talked about in this chapter, you will be able to take some of the stress out of your vacation planning so you can actually have a good time.

Conclusion

Thank for making it through to the end of *lagom*, let us hope it was informative, providing you with all the tools you need to achieve your goals - whatever they may be.

The next step is to decide how you would like to implement the ideas of lagom that we have discussed in this guidebook. There are so many different ways that you are able to do this! Learning the right steps, and how to make them work for you, can take some time and some dedication. However, with a good plan in place - and possibly starting with one step at a time – you can make this happen and live a life that you deeply enjoy.

The ideas of lagom are not groundbreaking - or even that hard to do. However, we live in a society where consumerism is the norm and where people are always competing to buy the latest thing and to own more of what they do not really need. This leads to a lot of clutter, a lot of extra work that is not needed; it also leads to a country full of people with no friends, too much work, and a lot of stress, and stuff that does not make them happy at all.

If you are tired of this kind of lifestyle and you are looking for a way to reduce the stress, improve your mental and physical wellbeing, and to ensure that you are getting the most out of your life, then lagom may be the answer for you. In addition, this guidebook has spent some time looking at the various steps that you can take in order to get this done.

When you are ready to simplify your life, ensure that you are gaining more happiness and enjoyment out of your life than ever before, and simplify your life all at the same time, make sure to check out this guidebook to help you get started with lagom.

Finally, if you found this book useful in any way, a review on Amazon is always appreciated!

Check out another book by Barbara Hayden

Printed in Great Britain
by Amazon